Mastering

Fujifilm X-T5

The Comprehensive Guide to Unlocking the Full Potential of your Camera from Creating Stunning Portraits to Breathtaking Landscapes

TABLE OF CONTENTS

xiii

INTRODUCTION

In 2014, Fujifilm unveiled the X-T1, a milestone release commemorating the company's 80th anniversary. This pioneering camera not only marked a celebratory moment but also sparked a profound transformation in the landscape of mirrorless and compact photography. Fast forward a decade and through five iterations, Fujifilm proudly introduces the latest addition to its esteemed X Series – a mirrorless digital camera that embodies the essence of timeless photography while delivering unparalleled image excellence.

The new Fujifilm X-T5 sets a new standard with its promise of unmatched picture quality, boasting features that redefine the boundaries of creativity. With a remarkable shutter speed of 1/180000sec and a standard sensitivity of ISO 125, photographers are equipped to capture moments with precision and clarity. Additionally, the innovative Pixel Shift Multi-Shot functionality opens up a realm of possibilities, empowering users to explore new dimensions in their photographic endeavors.

Harkening back to its origins, Fujifilm pays homage to its heritage by incorporating a 40-megapixel sensor and adorning the camera with a retro-style casing. This fusion of cutting-edge technology and timeless design principles ensures that the X-T5 stands as a testament to Fujifilm's legacy of innovation and craftsmanship. Moreover, cherished in-camera processing capabilities further elevate the photographic experience, allowing users to achieve stunning results straight out of the camera.

The Fujifilm X-T5 marks a triumphant return to the roots of the X-T series, embracing a more photogenic aesthetic that is sure to resonate with aficionados of dial-based controls. However, while this dedication to tradition is commendable, some adjustments to the body design may limit the camera's versatility compared to its predecessor, the X-T4. Nonetheless, with its unparalleled image quality and timeless design, the X-T5 is poised to inspire a new generation of photographers and reaffirm Fujifilm's position as a pioneer in the world of mirrorless photography.

OVERVIEW OF THE FUJIFILM X-T5 CAMERA

The Fujifilm X-T5 is a mirrorless camera with a 40-megapixel APSC sensor, 6.2k video, built-in stabilization, a tilting screen, and the familiar control buttons like the older models. It comes in silver or black color. Announced in November 2022, the X-T5 is the newest handheld digital camera in the X Series. These X- X-X-series cameras are known for having small, light bodies and producing high-quality images. The X-T5's powerful image-making capabilities guarantee that it is always prepared for action, irrespective of the subject's speed. With a maximum electronic shutter speed of 1/180,000 sec and a maximum mechanical shutter speed of 1/8000 sec, any subject can be stopped in its track. Additionally, the shutter release button provides an almost instantaneous response with a lag time of 35 Ms. Using the mechanical shutter, the X-T5 can capture images at a rate of 15fps, while the electronic shutter enables the capture of images at 20fps. The NP-W235 battery provides the capability to capture a maximum of 680 frames on a single charge. Additionally, the mechanical shutter ensures 500,000 actuations, thereby ensuring long-term accuracy and reliability. Aimed primarily at still photographers, the new X-T5 strikes an almost ideal balance between technical chops and that ill-defined thing photographers call "character.". The X-T5 is splash and dust-resistant, and although Fuji does not officially assign it an IP rating, it can be used with a sealed lens in harsh weather conditions. Although the X-T5 is available as a body only, it is also available in a kit with a lens. It is offered for $2,099 with the XF 18-55mm F2.8-4 and for $2,199 with the weather-protected XF 16-80mm F4. The Black and Silver Fujifilm X-T5 are priced at £1699 and $1799, respectively, for the camera body only in the United Kingdom and the United States.

Pros

- It is more compact than full frame camera
- Captivating 40MP images.
- It maintains the distinctive color science of Fujifilm, which includes film simulations.

- The dials and knobs make navigating this camera effortless and pleasurable.
- It has a great video feature.
- It has a good battery life (using the identical battery as the X-T4).
- It is built of magnesium and protected from dust and splashes
- Sensor 5-axis stabilization.
- It has a big, detailed, and clear EVF.
- It has a fully realized lens system

Cons

- Focus allows you to choose a subject type to get the best results.
- Rolling shutter distortion can be seen in video and e-shutter.
- For 160MP multi-shot mode to work, the scene must be completely still.
- Unable to contend with full-frame cameras in extremely low light.
- The viewfinder is also small compared to bigger cameras.
- There is no vertical battery grip option

Fujifilm X-T5 Specification

The dimensions of this camera are 3.6 by 5.1 by 2.52 inches (130 mm x 91 mm x 64 mm).

- It weighs 1.2 lb./ 557g including the battery
- Its body type is SLR-style mirrorless.
- Its sensor resolution is 40MP
- Its sensor type is X-Trans BSI CMOS
- The sensor size is APS-C
- The Lens Mount is a Fujifilm X
- It has 2 Memory card slots and SDXC (UHS-II) memory card format
- Its battery type is Fujifilm NP-W235
- The minimum and maximum ISO is 64 and 51200
- Its stabilization is 5-Axis IBIS
- It has a display screen size of 3 inches and a display resolution of 1.08 million dots
- The viewfinder type is EVF (Electronic View Finder) and viewfinder magnification is 0.8x with an EVF resolution of 3.7 million dots
- **Connectivity:** It can be connected through Bluetooth, Wi-Fi, USB-C, USB 3.2 Gen, micro-HDMI, Microphone (3.5mm), Remote (2.5mm), and PC Sync
- It has a Video resolution of 6.2K
- Its maximum shutter speed is 1/180,000 seconds and its minimum is 1/32000 seconds
- Processor is X-Processor 5
- White balance presets are 7
- The uncompressed format is RAW

- JPEG quality levels are Fine and Normal
- It has the aperture priority, shutter priority, manual exposure mode, and no subject/scene modes.
- It has no built-in flash but has an external flash via hot shoe.
- **Exposure compensation:** ±5 (at 1/3 EV steps)
- AE Bracketing: +3 (2, 3, 5, 7 frames at 1/3 EV, 2/3 EV, 1 EV, 2 EV steps)
- As we proceed to discuss the features, you will get familiar with more specifications of this amazing camera.

Body and Controls

The Fujifilm X-T5 looks like its predecessor, but it's a little smaller and has a more finger-shaped depression at the top of the hand grip and a less steep rise to the viewfinder hump, but still looks like a standard SLR. Like older X-T models, it has separate dials for shutter speed, ISO, and exposure compensation. Two command buttons on the front and rear of the camera can be programmed to perform similar functions. When you press either of the command dials, they can be used as function buttons or change the dial's function.

On the front of the body is a control for the AF mode that wasn't on the most current X-H2 models. The X-T5 still has a 3.64M dot OLED viewfinder, but it uses the X-H2's higher magnification optics, which gives it an amazing 0.8x equivalent magnification. In "Boost" mode, the finder can work at up to 100 frames per second, which is slower than the X-H2's 120 frames per second. Along with the dials on top, there is a drive mode switch under the ISO dial, and there is a function button on the front that allows you to change the specific options for this switch. To control the focusing mode, there is a focus mode switch on the front, and there is a joystick on the back that allows you to adjust the focus area.

Then to the bottom of the camera, there is no expansion port to add a vertical grip, so if that's something you need, you'll have to look at an X-H2. The X-T5 has the same NP-W235 batteries as the X-T4. It has a 16Wh battery that lets you take 590 pictures with the lens and 580 pictures with the rear screen on a single charge. If you turn on Boost mode and speed up the view to 100 frames per second or the rear screen to 60 frames per second, these numbers drop to 500 and 570 shots, respectively. The left and right keys control the film simulation and white balance modes, respectively, while the down key changes between the cameras boost modes, which makes the live view feed work better in different shooting situations. It's fantastic that this function is so basic to locate. On the majority of cameras, it is deep down the menus. The X-T5 doesn't have a headphone socket, and it sends video through a mini-HDMI port. With the USB adapter that comes in the box, you can output audio. With a magnesium metal shell and weatherproof construction, the body feels very strong in your hand. This camera from Fujifilm still has a retro look, but the handgrip has been improved so that it feels safe and solid even though it looks small.

CHAPTER 1

X-T5 FEATURES

The Fujifilm X-T5 is one of the company's finest cameras to date. Depending on the photographer, it could even be the most beneficial camera to purchase at this time. It's the X-T series' return to better photo quality, and photographers who like the dial-based settings should be happy with it. This camera is ideal for those who like manual settings, the distinctive color and style of Fujifilm's X series cameras, and the classic film camera ergonomics. Therefore, this chapter is going to discuss the features of this camera.

Still

One feature of this camera is the small and light body of this camera making it ideal for still photographers. Also, the Fujifilm XT5 has a switch under the shutter speed dial that lets you choose between stills and movie shooting. This camera can be used for both photography and video.

By using the Still/Movie switch, which toggles between dedicated in-camera menu systems, one can effortlessly switch from photography to the other options. The menu system for both Still/Movie is exceptionally well-organized. The Fujifilm X-T5 is, in essence, the most proficient and one of the most enjoyable APS-C cameras for still photographers.

Video

Another key feature of the Fujifilm X-T5 is its video quality. The X-T5 provides video at greater resolutions and of superior quality. There are up to 13+ stops of dynamic range in 4:2:2 10-bit video that the X-T5 records. There's also a 4K HQ mode that oversamples 6.2K footage for better 4K output. This higher video resolution unlocks 2x digital zoom functionality, giving you additional camera versatility without affecting the image quality. You can also record in both F-Log and F-Log2 formats, with F-Log2 giving you a wider dynamic range of 13+ stops. In addition, 12-bit ProRes RAW and Blackmagic RAW can be sent to Atomos and Blackmagic devices via HDMI.

Speed- Sensor, Processor

The X-T5's robust image-making capabilities guarantee that it is always prepared for action, irrespective of the subject's speed. With a maximum electronic shutter speed of 1/180,000 sec and a maximum mechanical shutter speed of 1/8000 sec, any subject can be abruptly stopped. Additionally, a latency time of 35 Ms ensures an almost instantaneous response upon pressing the shutter release button. With the mechanical shutter, the X-T5 can record images at a maximum rate of 15 fps, while the electronic shutter allows for 20 fps. In any case, every significant moment will be captured. A significant innovation of the X-T5 is its new image sensor. Featuring the highest resolution ever implemented in an X-T series camera, the sensor is predominantly intended for slow-motion subjects such as landscapes and portraits. The default ISO of the X-T5 ranges from 125 to 12,800 within its native frequency range. For more flexibility, the extended range goes from ISO 64 to 51,200.

Stabilization

The camera's in-body image stabilization (IBIS) system effectively reduces camera shaking, which is detrimental to image quality. This Built-in 5-axis sensor-shift image stabilization reduces camera shake up to 7 stops. This system is compatible with the majority of X Series lenses, including those that lack stabilization, and beneficial when shooting under challenging illumination conditions and with slower shutter speeds. Moreover, digital image stabilization can be used during video recording to maintain the stability of footage, particularly when recording handheld

EVF, LCD, AND TOUCH

Mega Electronic Viewfinder

Another feature is the mega electronic viewfinder which has a sharp 3.69m-dot resolution that lets you see things, brightly, and with great detail at eye level. It provides an easy-to-view image with a magnification of 0.8x, which is characterized by enhanced parallax and distortion suppression in comparison to its antecedent. In contrast, the 100-fps refresh rate enables the creation of images with minimal blackouts.

LCD- Keep the Mud off your Knees

Another feature is the three-way tilting LCD which gives you more options, especially when you're working at waist level or in portrait mode. The tilting LCD and center viewfinder align the lens, camera, and photographer on the optical axis, making taking pictures more comfortable and easier to understand.

Touch Screen

The LCD screen can also be used as a touch screen. The large 3.0" 1.62m-dot LCD touchscreen makes operation and playback easy, and the tilting design makes it much easier to work from both high and low shot angles. The X-T5's 3.0-inch rotating touchscreen has a higher resolution (up to 1.84 million dots). It is possible to move the focus point around with your thumb on the screen while looking through the lens on the X-T5. You can also tap an autofocus point to take a picture during this process.

Sport Finder Mode

The sports finder mode is a new feature that shows a 1.25x cropped frame on the screen and saves what's inside the frame. This makes it easier to take pictures of moving objects. That is to say, a 1.25× crop decreases the angle of view by an amount equivalent to a 1.25× increase in the focal length of the lens. The crop is represented by a frame in the display. When shooting and checking the subject in the viewfinder, you can see it just before it hits the frame. With the mechanical shutter, you can minimize the blackout time, which makes it useful for sports and wildlife photography.

Focus Brilliance

Autofocus

With its exceptional autofocus performance, the X-T5 now has a sensitivity of -7 EV and 425 phase-detection points, enabling it to function in extremely low-light conditions. Additionally, supported by deep learning and an AI adaptive algorithm, this focusing system can detect and track moving subjects, athletes, birds, automobiles, motorcycles, and animals with greater ease.

Focus Tracking & AF-C Custom Preset

In terms of focus tracking, the X-T5 exhibits remarkable speed and precision. The greater pixel count of the X-T5 enhances the quantity of phase detection pixels, thereby enhancing the accuracy of AF-S focusing on various subjects, such as portraits and landscapes. Additionally, a newly developed AF prediction algorithm for the X-H2S is integrated into the camera, allowing for stable focusing even when employing AF-C.

Subject Detection and Uprated Face Detection

The X-T5 can now automatically detect and track a wide range of things, such as animals, birds, cars, motorcycles, bicycles, airplanes, and trains. It can also do a great job of tracking and detecting human faces and eyes. This lets shooters focus on composition and creativity, knowing that the X-T5 will keep track of focus accurately.

Focus Zoom

Focus Zoom works in AF-S Single Point Autofocus Mode and Manual focus. This function enables you to rapidly concentrate on a selected object in manual focus mode and enlarge the designated focus region as the focus ring is rotated.

Pre-Shot ES (Burst) - Action Bracketing

The X-T5 has a smart Pre-shot burst shooting mode that helps you captures the exact moment. While you half-press the shutter button, the camera constantly fills the buffer with photos, and it then stores the most recent ones taken 0.5 to 1 second before you fully press the shutter button, so there is no delay caused by the camera or you. It is important to note that this function only works with the electronic shutter. Depending on whether you use a 1.29x crop or save photos that aren't cropped, you can get up to 15 to 20 frames per second for burst pictures. Which is fast, but not really that fast when you consider that some cameras can take 30 or even 60 shots per second with their electronic shutters.

Joystick and the AF Area - The Focus Lever

Fujifilm changed how the joystick works with X-T5, which gave us more settings for the focus button. To re-center the focus point on the X-T4 and many other X cameras, you just click the joystick once to enter the Focus Point Display View and then click it again to bring it back to the center. On the X-T5, you still click the joystick to enter the Focus Point Display View and edit or move your AF point, but you have to click the Disp/Back button (not the joystick) to re-center it.

Pixel-Shift

Fujifilm X-T5 features Pixel Shift Multi-Shot and the Pixel Shift Combiner software which work together to make a single ultralight resolution160MP picture with just one press of the shutter button. The X-T5 takes 20 exact pictures to make sure that each red, green, and blue pixel has the same information. It does this by shifting the sensor by a half pixel between each frame using in-body image stabilization. The result is a picture that has almost no false colors left. Then, go to Fujifilm.com and download the Pixel Shift Combiner software. Pick out the 20 files that make up each Pixel Shift shot, and the software will combine them into a single DNG file for you.

Nostalgic Neg. (Film Simulation)

Film Simulation modes enable the recreation of the appearance and texture of a variety of FUJIFILM film varieties. With its 19 Film Simulation modes, the X-T5 digitally reproduces the appearance of Fujifilm's classic photographic film stocks, which have been in production for over 85 years. They include Provia, Velvia, Astia, Classic Chrome, and PRO Neg. Std, PRO Neg. Hi, Classic Neg., Nostalgic Neg., Eterna Cinema, Eterna Bleach Bypass, Acros, Acros + Ye Filter, Acros + R Filter, Acros + G Filter, Black & White, Black & White + Ye Filter, Black & White + R Filter, Black & White + G Filter, and Sepia.

Multiple Exposures (9 Shots)

The next feature is the multiple exposures, which enable the combination of up to 9 consecutive images according to the Additive, Average, Light, or Dark rules. The X-T5 shows the composite thus far, which facilitates framing, and allows you to retake the previous photo if it failed. However, turning off the camera prevents you from loading a previous image from the card and also loses the composite so far.

HDR (High Dynamic Range)

Five different High Dynamic Range settings are available on the Fujifilm X-T5: AUTO, 200%, 400%, 800%, and 800%+. The camera takes three pictures, each with a different exposure because the shutter speed is different. It then combines them all in the came

CHAPTER 2

OTHER SIGNIFICANT FEATURES

The Fujifilm X-T5 adds several key significant features to its existing features which will be detailed in this chapter.

Photo Shooting Mode- Drive

This X-T5 offers modes of AE (auto exposure) to the user, which are aperture priority A, shutter priority S as well as program AE P. Mostly, to set AE, what people use is an aperture ring on lenses and shutter speed dial on the camera body to adjust these modes. However, the XT5's shooting modes are P (Program AE [auto exposure], S (Shutter Speed Priority, T (Time), B (Bulb), A (Aperture Priority), and M (Manual).

Customization

There are countless ways in which you can customize the X-T5 to tweak your preferences to get the most out of it, from buttons and screen displays to the different imaging modes among many others. Still, mode is capable of adjusting seven settings but you can only modify seven parameters in video mode. You can call all these elements "customization. "Now let's examine some of these.

The "Q" button

By pressing "Q" (Quick), one can access and modify the camera's settings. The Q Menu provides quick access to information and camera settings. Additionally, you can modify the contents of the Q Menu screen to suit your working style. With the Q button, you can access up to 16 different options which are customizable and quick to change as the name implies.

Function button

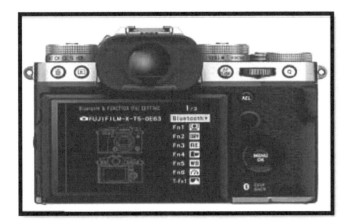

The function button is used to give different controls different functions. One of the best ways to make your Fuji fit your shooting style and make you more productive is to use the Function (Fn) buttons. Give the function button a job to do so you can quickly get to the chosen feature. **The default settings for the six Function (Fn) keys on the X-T5 are as follows.**

- Fn1: On/Off Face Detection: Activate or deactivate facial detection.
- Fn2: Drive Setting: To access the parameters used by each of the Drive modes.
- Fn3: Photometry (Metering Mode): Configures the camera's metering mode.
- Fn4: Film Simulation: Select a Film Simulation for the image to be applied to.
- Fn5: White Balance: To access the White Balance menu.
- Fn6: Performance: To toggle between Boost (faster AF speed and viewfinder display), Normal (standard AF speed and viewfinder display), and Economy (which restricts AF and viewfinder performance but consumes less battery power), press and hold the Performance button.

My Menu- Customize your menu

My menu is another custom menu that appears at the very bottom of the menu page when you press the menu button on the back of the camera. My menu is designed so that all of your most-used menu items can be found on one or two pages. It is empty by default, but you can add as many or as few choices as you need to fit your workflow and then rank them in terms of how important they are.

Other Customizations

Customizing EVF and LCD Information

The information that is displayed during scene composition can be modified to display only the desired data.

Customizing Film Simulation Modes

You probably already know about your camera's Film Simulation modes, but did you know that you can also make picture settings that suit your tastes by changing the color and contrast? With the H Tone, S Tone, and Color choices, you can change the brightness, contrast, and saturation of the colors. To make the changes, use the menu dial on the back. You can make a special preset of these new settings so you can quickly get back to them.

Flash

Another significant feature of the Fujifilm X-T5 is the use of flash which helps in illumination.

In addition to Fujifilm-branded or Fujifilm-compatible TTL flash units, generic third-party flash units may also be used. Almost anything that can be affixed to the hot shoe will function. When generic third-party flash units are used, TTL flash metering is no longer accessible; therefore, the power output of the flash must be adjusted manually. Additionally, automatic flash units with built-in light sensors that measure and regulate the flash output autonomously and separate from the camera are also available. Some best Flash for Fujifilm X-T5 are Fujifilm EF-60 Shoe Mount Flash suitable for either TTL or manual applications and can be used on or off camera, Godox V1 PRO, Fujifilm EF-42 Flash offering TTL flash metering support with tilting upward 90° and rotation 120° right and 180° left, for full control over light placement, Fujifilm EF-X20 which offers a guide number of 66' at ISO 100 and the 28mm (full frame) setting, etc.

Flash Sync Speed- 250k

The mechanical shutter of the X-T5 achieves a flash synchronization speed of 1/250 second, while the electronic shutter operates at 1/125 second. To further reduce the camera's visibility, the Silent menu option deactivates the flash, speaker, AF-assist lamp, and most significantly, the shutter-release sound, when the electronic shutter is engaged. This feature immediately renders the X-T5 ideal for more candid photography. The flash and shutter will synchronize at shutter velocities equal to or less than 1/250 second.

Inbuilt Films- Film Simulation

Fujifilm still has great color processing built right into the camera, and the 19 Film Simulation modes give you a lot of different looks to choose from. These days, you can save files in the 10-bit HEIF format, which should be better quality than regular JPEGs. But this isn't completely true yet because HEIF doesn't have a lot of software support.

Advanced Filter Set

Advanced Filters are the category that includes creative effect filters. Before making the shot, the Fujifilm X-T5 offers you the ability to view a sample of the 13 different creative filter effects on the LCD screen or in the EVF. Toys Cameras, Miniature, Pop Color, High-Key, Low-Key, Dynamic Tone, Soft Focus, Partial Color (Red), Partial Color (Orange), Partial Color (Yellow), Partial Color (Green), Partial Color (Blue), and Partial Color (Purple) are some of its effects.

Panorama

Filters like advanced and Panorama mode are available which combine individual photos to make a very wide or a very tall image. This panorama effect is created through the combining of several pictures to make a broader scene. Most of the time panoramic views portray a wide expanse of scenes with changing light and distinct shades.

Hybrid Shutter - Mechanical, Electrical, Front Curtain

The X-T5 has two types of shutters: there will be an electric shutter and a mechanical one, too. In all shooting situations fast shutter speed that the mechanical focal-plane shutter can be used is 1/8000th second. Because there is no ND filter at all, you can buy a real glass ND filter that will be able to provide you with the mechanical shutter if you need to use a very fast lens with the mechanical shutter in very bright sunlight. The topmost shutter speed for the electronic shutter is 2.5 stops faster, going from 1/32000 sec on the former XT4 to a phenomenal 1/180000 sec on the new XT5.

Wireless- Wi-Fi, Bluetooth

The X-T5 Fujifilm model is equipped with built-in Wi-Fi and Bluetooth, and the current app which allows the addition of location details from your phone works fine with them. With the Fujifilm Camera Remote App, your phone becomes a remote control of your camera. Once done, you can move the photos to your phone and post them on any social media site. The shutter release is another function that can be done through Bluetooth with your phone. It is wireless and can be used for live view and also for fine adjustment of the camera settings. In-built Bluetooth and Wi-Fi support enables you to share pictures wirelessly to your phone or even operate the camera from your phone remotely.

Lens Correction

Some camera manufacturers rely on specific correction profiles that must be provided by each RAW converter maker. Fujifilm is not one of these companies. Instead, all contemporary Fujifilm cameras save digital corrections as information within the RAW file. RAW converters can access lens-specific metadata and use it to make necessary repairs. This allows the built-in RAW converter and external RAW conversion software, such as Adobe Lightroom or Capture One, to use the RAW file's metadata to correct or lessen vignetting, distortion, and chromatic aberration. Most contemporary lenses achieve their highest image quality by combining optical and digital adjustments.

Corrections are mostly used for the three following phenomena:

- **Vignetting:** This effect causes a reduction of brightness from center to corner. Vignetting is more noticeable with larger (open) apertures.
- **Distortion:** Pincushion- and barrel-type distortions [18] make straight lines appear bent. Some prime lenses, including the XF14mm, XF23mmF2, XF35mmF1.4, XF56mm (old and new), and XF90mm, are entirely optically corrected for distortion
- **Chromatic aberration causes color fringing.** This effect can be addressed (or lessened) with apochromatic lenses or digitally during RAW conversion.

CHAPTER 3

CAMERA CONFIGURATION

Essential Configuration

The first step is attaching the strap to the camera that was just unboxed. Link the strap fasteners to the strap clip. In order not to let the camera fall, make sure that the strap is tightened properly.

The next is to insert the lenses. It is possible to use an X-mount lens on the camera Fujifilm. Remove the rear lens cap and body cap of the camera. First of all, place the lens on the mount by lining up the markings on the lens and the camera. Then, turn the lens until it clicks into place.

Battery should be inserted next. For this reason, you should remove the battery cover first.

Now, move the cover of the battery chamber by sliding the latch on the cover over the battery chamber.

Then put the battery in, and close the battery chamber.

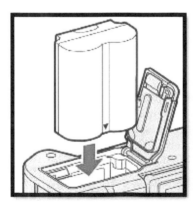

Note: The camera comes with a rechargeable NP-W235 battery. The process takes about 180 minutes to charge the battery fully.

The next step is to insert the memory card. Open your memory card slot cover, put the card in, and then close the cover.

Afterwards, turn on the camera by turning the switch ON/OFF. At the very start, the camera allows you to select your language of communication. Choose a language and press MENU/OK on the remote controller.

Afterward, a time zone. Select a time zone and toggle daylight saving time on or off using the selector when prompted, then press MENU/OK after selecting SET.

Next is to set the clock.

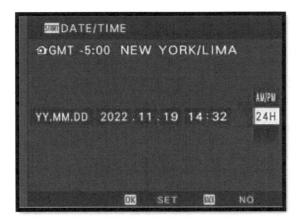

Next, view the details on the smartphone app. The camera will show you a QR code that you can scan with your phone to go to a website where you can download the smartphone application. To exit the shooting screen, press MENU/OK.

Finally, you can decide to format the memory card. Before using memory cards for the first time, format them, and ensure that they are all formatted again before inserting them into a computer or other device.

Customizing Camera Function

It is important to make sure that frequently used features are assigned to Fn buttons that are easy to reach so that shooting goes smoothly and without any problems. However, the number of available buttons is limited. Luckily, we have My Menu and the Quick menu (Q button) to quickly access frequently used functions and menus that don't fit into the Fn button lineup.

Customizing Fn button and Gestures

The Fn and Touch-Fn buttons on the X-T5 will save you a lot of time and stress going to the camera app. Assign each function button or touch function a role so you can quickly access the feature you want.

To assign roles to the Function Button:

- Click the menu button.
- Press the setup menu button/dial setting.

- Next, select the function (Fn) setting.

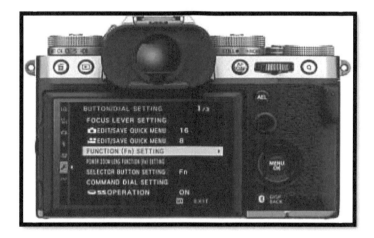

Note: One quick way to see the function (Fn) setting is to press and hold the DISP/BACK button until a control selection menu appears.

Simply scroll through the list and choose the control that you want to change. You see a list of all the functions that can be assigned to that control when you press OK.

Touch-Function Gestures

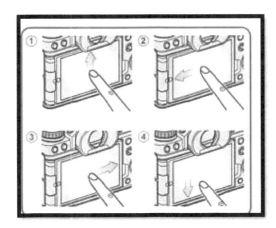

The touch function simply means using your fingers to operate on the screen. By flicking the monitor, you can get to the tasks that are assigned to T-Fn1 through T-Fn4.

Note: By default, touch-function gestures are disabled.

To enable touch-function gestures: In the menu, navigate to "Setup" and then "Button/Daily Setting."

Next, select the touchscreen setting

Then navigate to the touch screen setting

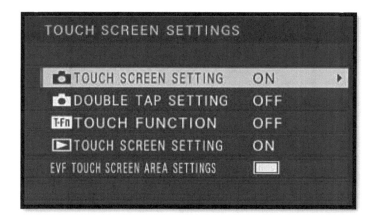

Turn it on and assign distinct keys to the functions. Depending on the setting, the desired button can be selected using only the finger.

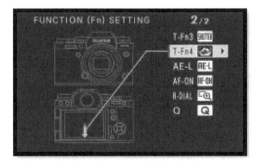

The Q Menu

The Q button allows you to quickly access frequently used buttons on your camera. Press Q to display the quick menu during shooting.

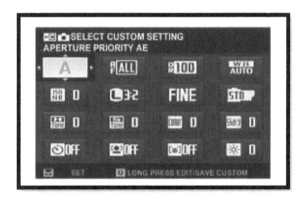

Use the selector to highlight items and rotate the rear command dial to change. The quick menu shows the options currently selected for items

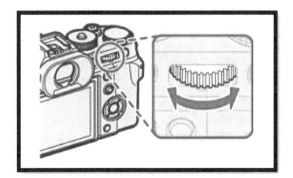

Press Ok after selecting the preferred item to assign it to the selected position and press the Q button to exit when settings are complete. To edit or change an item, press and hold the Q button during shooting, the current quick menu will be displayed; use the selector to highlight the item you wish to change and press MENU/OK. Highlight any of the options and press MENU/OK to assign it to the selected position.

Custom Settings (C1-C7)

Another thing we can customize is the custom settings or film recipes. You can take those film simulations and further customize them to your liking by adjusting color, contrast, and more which are going to give you your styling options. For example, if you want a very vivid contrast style for landscapes, you can create a landscape preset and then if you're going to photograph a portrait right after that landscape you can go to your portrait preset which might have some more muted colors and softer contrast.

Note: With this camera, you can save things like your settings and focus settings.

To create a custom setting, select IMAGE QUALITY SETTING > EDIT/SAVE CUSTOM SETTING > CREATE NEW at one of the seven available slots. This saves your current camera settings in this slot. You can name a custom setting by selecting it and choosing EDIT CUSTOM SETTING.

Sadly, the X-T5 stops short of saving all camera settings in a custom setting slot. To see what parameters can be saved, you can create a new one or select an existing custom setting with IMAGE QUALITY SETTING > EDIT/SAVE CUSTOM SETTING and then pick EDIT/CHECK. The camera will now show you all the available menu items. Items that cannot be saved in custom settings are grayed out. In addition to this, you cannot save settings that can also be accessed via "analog" dials and switches. These settings are aperture, shutter speed, ISO, exposure compensation, DRIVE mode, STILL/MOVIE mode, and focus mode. To activate a specific custom setting, you can either visit the Quick menu or use IMAGE QUALITY SETTING > SELECT CUSTOM SETTING. You can also assign the custom settings selection to an Fn button (SELECT CUSTOM SETTING) or configure an Fn button to immediately select Custom Setting 1 when that button is pressed (RECALL CUSTOM 1 SETTING). The latter can be helpful in situations that require you to immediately switch to a different camera configuration, for example, one for sudden action shot opportunities. To reassign Fn buttons, press and hold the DISP/BACK button until the configuration page appears. Press OK and follow the confirmation dialog to save the current settings.

Then press OK.

My Menu

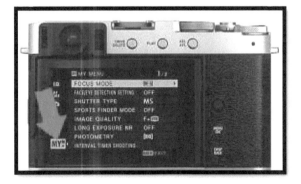

To configure My Menu, select SET UP > USER SETTING >MY MENU SETTING, where you can add new items, rank existing items (i.e., change their position in My Menu), or remove items from the menu.

Working with the Display

This section lists the indicators that may be displayed during shooting.

Display View

Electronic Viewfinder

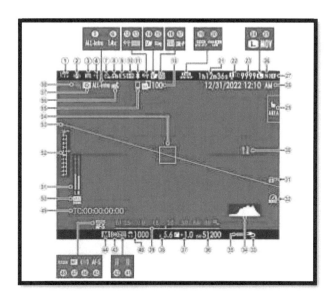

- **The Crop Mode:** It shows the present crop.
- **IS (Image Stabilization) Mode:** You can set the image stabilization to Always On, Shooting only (only works in Focus mode C or when the shutter is released), or off.
- **Flash (TTL) Mode:** This mode shows the TTL for a flash that stands on a hot-shoe-mounted flash.
- **Flash Compensation:** This button displays the present amount of flash compensation.
- **Movie Compression:** This shows the movie compression that is currently being used.
- **Digital Teleconverter:** This button is the button that shows if the digital teleconverter is on (1.4x or 2.0x).
- **Self-Timer Indicator:** This indicates the number of seconds remaining before taking the shot.
- **Continuous Mode:** This button lets you know which of the two continuous modes (CH (Continuous High) or CL (Continuous Low)) is selected.
- **Shutter Type:** This implies the type of shutter that is selected and what the impact will be on the aesthetics of the building.
- **AF+MF indicator:** This button shows you if AF+MF is active or not.
- **Bluetooth ON/OFF:** This button allows you to check if Bluetooth is On or Off.
- **White Balance:** This is where it is possible to check the current White Balance setting.
- **AWB Lock:** This button will make you aware if AWB is locked.
- Film Simulation: This shows the Film Simulation that is currently chosen.
- **F-Log/HLG Recording:** This button lets you know whether F-Log or HLG (Hybrid Log-Gamma) is being used.
- **Dynamic Range:** This button shows the setting for dynamic range.
- **Priority:** This shows the D-Range setting.
- **Image Transfer state:** This shows the state of the current image transfer.
- **Movie Mode:** The movie mode is shown, along with the frame rate, bit rate, frame size, and aspect ratio.
- **High-Speed Recording:** This shows the settings that are being used presently. This lets you play back videos in slow motion.
- **Recording Time Remaining / Elapsed Recording Time:** This can be used to know how much time is left to record or how much time has already been recorded.
- **Card Slot Options:** You can make memory cards work in different ways when you use two of them:
- **Number of Available Frames:** This number shows how many frames can still be taken with the available settings.
- **Image Size:** This shows the size of the present file.
- **File Format:** This is where you can see the current file format.
- **Image Quality:** This shows the quality of the image right now.
- **HEIF Format:** This shows when the HEIF format is being used.
- **Date and Time:** This helps to show the present date and time.
- **Touch Screen Mode:** This mode displays the selected touch screen control

- **Temperature Warning:** This shows up when the camera gets too hot. Wait for the camera to cool down before turning it back on.
- **Control Lock:** This button shows up when the Menu/OK button is pressed and held to lock the settings.
- **Boost Mode:** Boost Mode makes the screen and AF faster. This function is shown to be on or off.
- **Power Supply:** This shows when the camera is being charged via USB.
- **Battery Level:** This shows how much power the battery has.
- **Histogram:** This button displays the histogram for the present view.
- **Sensitivity (ISO):** This shows the current ISO.
- **Exposure Compensation:** This shows the exposure pay at the moment.
- **Aperture:** This shows the default aperture.
- **Distance Indicator:** This shows how far away the subject is.
- **Shutter Speed:** This shows the shutter speed at the moment.
- **TTL Lock:** This button lets you know when the Flash TTL output is locked. Lock with Last Flash or Lock with Metering Flash is used to make sure that output stays the same across a set of pictures.
- **AE Lock:** This button lets you know when the exposure is locked.
- **Metering:** This mode shows the current Metering mode.
- **Shooting Mode:** This lets you see the present shooting mode.
- **Focus Mode:** This shows the current Focus mode.
- **Focus Indicator:** This shows the state of the focus.
- **Manual Focus Indicator:** This button lets you know when you're in manual focus mode.
- **AF Lock:** This button lets you know when the AF is locked.
- **Time Code:** This shows the current time code.
- **Mic Input Channel:** This shows the current input channel.
- **Recording Level:** This shows the level of the current audio clip.
- **Exposure Indicator:** This shows when the camera is in M mode, how different the current settings are from what it thinks the right exposure should be for that mode.
- **Virtual Horizon:** This button shows the virtual horizon and lets you make pictures that are level.
- **Focus Check:** If this setting is chosen, the screen will get bigger when you turn the focus ring in Single AF (AF-S) or Manual focus mode.
- **Depth-of-Field Preview:** This shows when the Preview Depth of Field is on.
- **Location Data Download Status:** This shows the state of the data download at the moment.
- **Bluetooth Host:** This shows that the camera is linked to a smart device.
- **Focus Frame:** This shows the camera's focus area.

The LCD Monitor

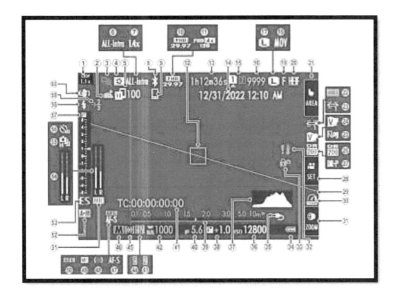

1. **Crop Mode:** This mode shows the current crop.

2. **Location Data Download status:** This shows the state of the data download at the moment.

3. **Focus Check:** If this setting is used, the screen will get bigger when you turn the focus ring in Single AF (AF-S) or Manual focus mode.

4. **Preview Depth of Field:** This shows when Preview Depth of Field is on.

5. **Image Transfer status:** This shows the state of the image transfer at the moment.

6. **Movie Compression:** This shows the movie compression that is currently being used.

7. **Digital Teleconverter:** This button lets you see if the digital teleconverter is on (1.4x or 2.0x).

8. **Bluetooth on/off:** You can see if the camera's Bluetooth is on or off.

9. **Bluetooth Host:** This feature lets you see when the camera is linked to a smart device.

10. **Movie Mode:** This button displays the current movie mode, including the frame rate, bit rate, frame size, and aspect ratio.

11. **High-Speed Recording:** This shows the settings that are being used right now. This lets you play back videos in slow motion.

12. **Focus Frame:** This shows the camera's focus area.

13. **Recording Time Remaining/Elapsed Recording Time:** This demonstrates the amount of time that is left or the amount of time that has already been used.

14. **Date and Time:** This shows the present date and time.

15. **Card Slot Options:** You can make the following memory cards work in different ways when you use two of them

16. **Number of Available Frames:** This number shows how many frames can still be taken with the current settings.

17. **Image Size:** This shows the size of the current image.

18. **File Format:** This button displays the current file format.

19. **Image Quality:** This shows the quality of the current image.
20. **HEIF Format:** This shows when the HEIF format is being used.
21. **Touch Screen Mode:** This mode displays the selected touch screen.
22. **AWB Lock:** This button is used to determine if the AWB is locked.
23. **White Balance:** This is the window that shows your current White Balance setting.
24. **Film Simulation:** This shows the Film Simulation that is currently chosen.
25. **The F-Log/HLG button** reminds you whether F-Log or HLG (Hybrid Log-Gamma) gamma is being applied.
26. **Dynamic Range:** This button shows the setting for dynamic range.
27. **D-Range Priority:** This shows the D-Range setting.
28. **Movie Optimized Control:** If you tap this, the dials and touch controls for making movies will change.
29. **Virtual Horizon:** This feature displays the virtual horizon and lets you make pictures that are level.
30. **Boost Mode makes the screen and AF faster.** This function is shown to be on or off.
31. **Touch Zoom:** If the lens lets you, you can tap the screen to make it bigger.
32. **Temperature Warning:** The temperature warning lets you know when the camera gets too hot. Wait for the camera to cool down before turning it back on.
33. **Control Lock:** This button lets you know when the keys have been locked by holding down the Menu/OK button.
34. **Battery Level:** This shows how much power the battery has.
35. **Power Supply:** This shows when the camera is being charged via USB.
36. **Sensitivity (ISO):** This shows the current ISO.
37. **Histogram:** This is where you can see the current view's histogram.
38. **Exposure compensation:** This shows the current exposure compensation.
39. **Distance Indicator:** This shows how far away the subject is.
40. **Aperture:** This shows the current aperture.
41. **Time Code:** It shows the time code at the moment.
42. **Shutter Speed:** This shows the shutter speed at the moment.
43. **TTL Lock:** This button lets you know when the Flash TTL output is locked. Lock with Last Flash or Lock with Metering Flash is used to make sure that output stays the same across a set of pictures.
44. **AE Lock:** This button lets you know when the exposure is locked.
45. **Metering:** This mode shows the current Metering method.
46. **Shooting Mode:** This lets you see the present shooting mode.
47. **Focus Mode:** This shows the current Focus mode.
48. **Focus Indicator:** This shows what the focus is on.
49. **Manual Focus Indicator:** This button will notify you when you switch to manual focus mode.
50. **AF Lock:** This button lets you know when the autofocus is set.
51. **Mic Input Channel:** This shows the current input channel.
52. **AF+MF Indicator:** This button lets you know if AF+MF is on or off.
53. **Shutter Type:** This shows what kind of shutter is chosen.

54. **Recording Level:** This shows the level of the current audio clip.

55. **Continuous Mode:** This shows which Continuous mode is chosen: CL (Continuous Low) or CH (Continuous High).

56. **Self-Timer Indicator:** This shows how many seconds are left until the camera takes a shot.

57. **Exposure Indicator:** This shows in M mode, how different the current settings are from what the camera thinks the right exposure should be for that mode.

58. **Flash (TTL) Mode:** This mode displays the TTL for a flash placed on a hot shoe.

59. **Flash Compensation:** This shows how much flash compensation is currently.

60. IS (Image Stabilization) Mode: You can set the image stabilization to Always On, Shooting only (only works in Focus mode C or when the shutter is released), or off.

Display Mode

The [VIEW MODE] button should be pressed to switch between the following displays modes. A record or playback mode can be set on the monitor.

To choose the display mode for the EVF and LCD, go to [SETUP] > [VIEW MODE SETTING] in the setup menu.

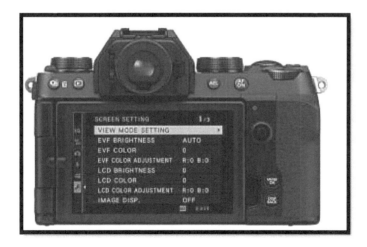

To switch between the Displays modes, just click the View Mode button.

- **Eye Sensor:** When you look through the viewfinder, the EVF turns on. At that moment, the LCD screen gets off. If you take your eye off the viewfinder, then the LCD screen goes on and the EVF turns off.
- **LCD Only:** The screen is LCD, but the EVF is off.
- **EVF Only:** The EVF is on, but the LCD screen is off.
- **EVF Only + Eye Sensor:** When you look away from the lens, the EVF turns on. When the eye is moved away, EVF goes off. The LCD monitor stays off.
- **Eye Sensor + LCD Image Display:** If you put your eye on the viewfinder while you're shooting, the EVF gets activated. Nevertheless, the LCD monitor is where the images are displayed even if you are not looking through the viewfinder after the shoot.

Adjusting Display Brightness

The [SCREEN SET-UP] menu offers options for changing the brightness and saturation of the viewfinder and LCD monitor. Pushing [EVF BRIGHTNESS] or [EVF COLOR] buttons allow you to adjust the brightness or saturation of the viewfinder. You can do this by pressing the LCD brightness or saturation keys.

Display Rotation

When [ON] is chosen for [SCREEN SET-UP] > [AUTOROTATE DISPLAYS], the LCD monitor and viewfinder indicators will automatically turn to match the camera position.

The [DISP/BACK] Button

The [DISP/BACK] button changes how the signs show up in the viewfinder and on the LCD screen.

Configuring the Custom Display

To configure the information that is shown on the standard indicator display, press the [DISP/BACK] button.

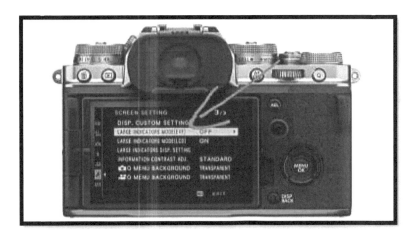

Select [SCREEN SET-UP] > [DISP. CUSTOM SETTING] in the setup menu.

- Choose items. And press [MENU/OK] to select or deselect.
- Press [DISP/BACK] to save changes.
- Press [DISP/BACK] as needed to exit the menus and return to the shooting display.

Dual Display View

There is a big full-frame window and a smaller close-up of the focus area on the dual display.

Working with the Touch Screen

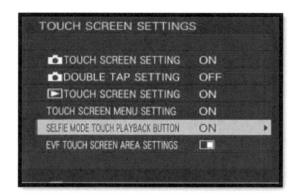

You can use touch controls to do things like pick out the center area and take pictures. You can choose the action that will be taken by hitting the display's touchscreen mode indicator to go through the following choices:

- The TOUCH SCREEN MODE choice in the shooting menu lets you change the settings for touch controls. When OFF is chosen for TOUCH SCREEN SETTING in the setup menu, the touch screen mode indicator is not shown and touch functions can't be used.
- The LCD screen can also be used as a touch screen.
- To use touch functions, go to [BUTTON/DIAL SETTING] > [TOUCH SCREEN SETTING] > [TOUCH SCREEN SETTING] and select [ON].

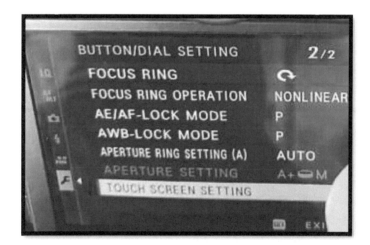

Shooting Stills with the Touch Screen

- **Touch Shooting Mode:** Tap your subject in the display to focus and release the shutter. In burst mode, pictures will be taken while you keep your finger on the display.
- **AF Mode:** Tap to select a focus point and lock focus. The shutter can be released by pressing the shutter button down.
- **AREA Mode:** Tap to select a point for focus or zoom. The focus frame will move to the selected point.
- **OFF:** Touch controls off. The display does not respond when tapped.

Shooting Movies with the Touch Screen

Making movies on the touchscreen

You can use the touchscreen to choose a focus frame or zone, autofocus with that frame or zone, or autofocus and shoot with that frame or zone. These are the choices you have:
- **AREA:** To choose a target frame or zone, tap the LCD screen once.
- **AF:** To start autofocus, tap on the LCD screen to choose a target frame or zone. This choice will use Instant AF to focus the camera when it is in MF mode.
- **SHOT:** Press and hold on to the touchscreen to choose a focus area or zone. The camera will then be activated through this frame or zone, and you can take a picture right away. This choice will take a picture right away in MF mode without (re-)focusing.
- **OFF:** Turns off the light with the touchscreen. This keeps you from accidentally using any of the other three tasks on the touchscreen.

Movie Optimized Control

When you go to [MOVIE SETTING] > [MOVIE OPTIMIZED CONTROL], choose [ON]. The command keys and touch controls are set up to work best for recording movies when you press the movie-optimized mode button on the shooting display or press OK. This can be used to stop sounds from the camera from being recorded with movie clips.
Note: The aperture ring and the shutter speed, sensitivity, and exposure correction dials are turned off when movie-optimized controls are turned on.
The movie-optimized mode button can be used to change the shooting settings or turn off movie-optimized control when it is turned on.

Playback Image with the Touch Screen

In addition to aiming and switching on the camera, the touch screen can do the following:

When the screen is in play mode, use it like a smartphone to slide through the pictures. By double-taping or pinching the picture with two fingers, you can also zoom in or out. To employ the touch screen for playback, navigate to SET UP > BUTTON/DIAL SETTING > TOUCH SCREEN SETTING > Playback. You can still use the touchscreen even when the electronic vision (EVF) is turned on. The touchscreen acts like a trackpad in this case, letting you move the current focus frame without seeing it. To set the touchscreen area that can be used for EVF operations, go to SET UP > BUTTON/DIAL SETTING > TOUCH SCREEN SETTING > EVF TOUCH SCREEN AREA SETTINGS. You can pick from seven active places or turn it off. A second tap on the screen will let you zoom in on a picture while taking or playing back. This function does the same thing as pressing the rear command key on the FOCUS CHECK position. To make sure you can use this feature while taking photos, go to SET UP > BUTTON/DIAL SETTING > TOUCH SCREEN SETTING > CAMERA SETTING > DOUBLE TAP > ON. When you are looking through the EVF, double tapping also works if you have set up a touchscreen spot for EVF use. Last but not least, the touchscreen lets you use four fake Fn buttons, which are also known as Touch-Fn or T-Fn buttons. If you move your finger left, right, up, or down on the screen, you can "press" one of these buttons. If you press and hold the DISP/BACK button until the FUNCTION (Fn) SETTING screen shows up, you can add new T-Fn features. When you go to SET UP > BUTTON/DIAL SETTING > TOUCH SCREEN SETTING > T-Fn TOUCH FUNCTION, make sure that the T-Fn TOUCH FUNCTION is turned on.

Touch controls can be used for the following playing tasks when [ON]:

- **Swipe:** To see other pictures, swipe your finger across the screen.
- **Pinch out:** To zoom in, use two fingers on the screen and spread them widely.
- **Pinch-in:** To zoom out, you should put two fingers on the screen and push them together.
- **Tap twice:** To get the center point better, tap the screen twice.
- **Drag:** During playback, you can zoom in on other parts of the picture.

Exercise

1. Describe the process of unboxing the camera to turning it on
2. What is the importance of the camera strap
3. How do you customize the function button
4. Write briefly about the Q button

CHAPTER 4

QUICK START GUIDE

Exposure Essentials- P S A M

Some camera parameters determine the brightness of the images captured with an X Series camera: the exposure, the shutter speed, the aperture, and the ISO. The camera's Auto Mode also continues to modify the three elements in the background electronically. Initially, you will need to try out the different adjustments in shutter speed, aperture, and ISO values to get the perfectly exposed – neither overexposed nor underexposed – shots. But in every scene, you will see many influential factors that will assist you in thinking out of the box and being more creative in your photography.

Let's have a closer look at each of these settings:

P (Program AE [auto exposure]): The camera sets the aperture and the shutter speed for optimal exposure. Press the A button on the Aperture and Shutter Speed set to A (auto), it should be visible from the P letter on the screen.

S (Shutter Speed Priority): This shutter speed mode is set by the photographer and the aperture is set by the camera such that the aperture is selected specifically for each shutter speed you select. It is indicated as S on the camera screen.

A (Aperture Priority): The camera's shutter is the camera function, whereas the aperture is set by the photographer. For that, rotate the aperture ring of the lens (anticlockwise) forward to the f/stop (marked on the lens) and set the User-Selected option (the icon of the aperture) on the lens aperture mode switch.

Manual (M): The aperture and the shutter speed are set by the person behind the camera. The aperture mode is selected through the lens aperture mode switch and the shutter speed is set through the Shutter Speed dial.

It is important to understand that these auto exposure (AE) modes (including Auto-ISO) are not responsible for correctly exposing images: exposure is always the responsibility of the photographer. AE modes automatically fill variables (such as the shutter speed in aperture priority A) in a way that matches the exposure you have set. Auto exposure will only deliver good results if the photographer is exposing correctly.

Focusing Essentials

The focus modes are adjusted via a dial located on the front of the camera.

How does the camera know what to focus on

The focus indicator helps in the determination of the moment to focus. The focus indicator blinks white when the camera is unable to focus and green when the subject is in focus. Brackets ("()") are continuously displayed in mode C to signify that the camera is focusing. "MF" indicates the use of manual focus.

Single AF/Continuous AF Focusing Mode

To adjust the Focus mode, Use the Focus Mode selector. **AF-S**, also known as single AF, starts to focus upon the press of the shutter button and locks it once focus is attained. Most suitable for stationary subjects. When using single autofocus, the camera will center its focus on the closest object within the designated area when the shutter button is half-pressed. You can then take the photo knowing that the subject is in sharp focus.

C: AF-C (Continuous AF): The focus starts midway through the press of the shutter button and remains in focus until the photograph is captured. The most effective for moving subjects. When continuous autofocus is enabled, half-pressing the shutter button will center the image on the closest object within the focus area. The camera will then continue to refocus on that point while the shutter button remains half-pressed

Instant AF and Back Button Focus

Instant AF enables the X-T5 to be autofocused in manual focus mode with the click of the AF-ON button. Instant AF operates consistently at a wide aperture. Although Instant AF is the most accurate AF method offered, it operates slightly more slowly than the standard autofocus of the camera. It is possible to combine it with manual focusing: after rapidly autofocusing on an object with Instant AF, the focus can be manually adjusted by rotating the focus ring and using MF assistants such as the magnifier and focus peaking.

Face/Eye Detection

The autofocus and exposure metering modes are combined for subject and face detection. Even the automatic white balance is affected. By selecting one of the four eye detection options from AF/MF SETTING > FACE/EYE DETECTION SETTING > FACE DETECTION ON, face/eye detection can be enabled.

Here's what it does:

Human faces, heads, and bodies are detected by the camera as it examines the scene. When half-pressing the shutter trigger, one of the detected subjects is automatically brought into focus. In situations where the camera detects multiple faces or individuals, it will typically concentrate on the one that is in closest proximity to the focus frame or zone of the underlying autofocus focus mode.

The different options are:

- **ENABLE FACE DETECTION:** Modify configurations to enable intelligent face detection.
- **EYE OFF:** Only intelligent face detection.
- **EYE AUTO:** When a face is detected, the camera automatically selects which eye to focus on.
- **RIGHT EYE PRIORITY:** When subjects are detected via Intelligent Face Detection, the camera focuses preferentially on the right eye.
- **LEFT EYE PRIORITY:** Priority for the left eye is given by the camera when subjects are detected via Intelligent Face Detection.
- **OFF:** Intelligent Face Detection and eye priority are disabled.
- **Eye/Face Detection** AF can be enabled via the camera's main menu; it is more conveniently accessible through the Q Menu, where it is pre-enabled.

You can cycle between four modes:

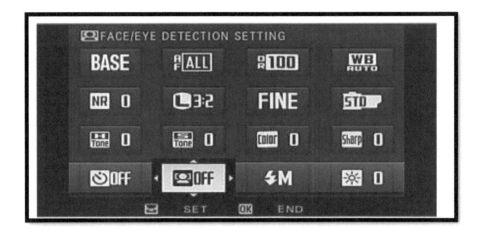

You may not think there is much difference between Face and Eye Detection, but if you're photographing a face-filling portrait with a very shallow depth-of-field, using one of the Eye Detection modes can make the difference between someone's eyes being in focus (the window to their soul, remember) or their nose being pin-sharp instead. You'll see detected faces in the viewfinder even before you've focused on them, highlighted with boxes. A green box highlights the face currently being tracked as a priority. If there are any other faces in the frame, these may be highlighted with white boxes. Some X Series cameras let you switch between which face is being tracked just by rotating the rear command dial, which is easy to do with the camera at your eye.

Subject Detection

Determine whether, when setting focus, the camera gives precedence to particular types of subjects, such as vehicles or creatures.

To activate subject detection, select one of the subject types enumerated below.

- ANIMAL: The camera monitors and detects the focus of dogs and cats.
- BIRD: Birds are detected and tracked by the camera.
- AUTOMOBILE: The camera detects and monitors the focus on the front ends or bodies of automobiles, predominantly those used in motorsports.
- MOTORCYCLE & BIKE: The camera detects and follows bicycle and motorcycle riders in focus.
- AIRPLANE: The camera is capable of detecting and tracking the focus of an aircraft on its nose, body, cockpit, or snout.

- TRAIN: The camera is capable of detecting and tracking train focus on the driver compartments or front extremities.
- OFF: Detection is deactivated.

Image Stabilization Essentials

Previously, when the camera technology was not advanced, the only option to get a shake-free image was to put the camera on a very stable tripod. While the camera was formerly attached to the tripod, the risk of camera shaking is reduced and as a result, quality images can be captured. Despite that, in the past years, image stabilizing technology has seen remarkable growth, which focuses on lessening the number of camera shake occasions while taking photos by hand. OIS and IBIS, the two primary stabilization methods, together, can help the camera to achieve its stabilizing effects. Here, we shall examine each of them in turn.

Optical Image Stabilization

OIS is a system found in Fujifilm XF, XC, and GF lenses. The purpose of OIS is to combat camera shake caused by horizontal or vertical movement. Thousands of calculations are performed per second by a series of gyroscopic sensors within the lens to determine when and how the lens is in motion. Then, one of the motorized lens elements is adjusted to counteract the movement. When the OIS system is active, an internal whirring can be heard through the lens. Although OIS is lens-dependent, an option exists on your camera to determine when OIS is active. From the menu labeled SHOOTING SETTINGS, select IS MODE.

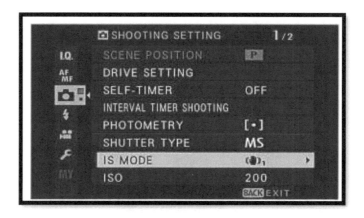

Here, two options will be presented to you: CONTINUOUS or SHOOTING ONLY. While the camera is powered on, the OIS system remains active under the CONTINUOUS setting. Focus Mode determines OIS system activation for the SHOOTING ONLY option. Lens stabilization is initiated in AF-S mode exclusively when the shutter is completely released, whereas it is initiated in AF-C mode when the shutter is pressed midway. To optimize battery life, select SHOOTING ONLY. This function operates on IBIS as well.

In-Body Image Stabilization (IBIS)

IBIS provides a sophisticated standard of image stabilization. This system demonstrates the capability to provide compensation of up to five stops, regardless of the lens being used. This is because the sensor of the camera is moved as opposed to a component within the lens being used to compensate for motion. Although IBIS is particularly great when capturing still images, it also demonstrates its prowess in handheld video footage by preventing "bouncing" during simultaneous filming and strolling.

When Not to Use Image Stabilization

Despite how good IBIS and OIS are, there will be situations in which you should avoid using them: WHEN YOU WANT TO MAXIMIZE BATTERY LIFE: IBIS and OIS are powered by batteries. Turn them off when the battery is low or when you want the longest possible time to create images.

WHEN SHOOTING VIDEO USING THE INTERNAL MICROPHONE: When using OIS or IBIS to record video, ensure that sound is captured using a distinct microphone or recorder. This is due to the likelihood that the internal microphone of the camera will detect the vibrations produced by the stabilization system while it operates.

Playback Essentials

During playback, the DISP/BACK button regulates the visibility of indicators. There are three options:

Standard

Information Off

Information Display

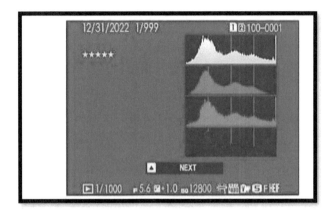

Note: The photo information display changes each time the selector is pressed up

Viewing Pictures

To go from full-frame playback to playback magnification or multi-frame playback, use the rear command dial.

- **Playback Zoom**: To enlarge the current image, rotate the rear command dial to the right; to enlarge it, rotate it to the left. To exit Zoom, select the center of the rear command dial, DISP/BACK, or MENU/OK.
- The maximum zoom ratio is dependent on the IMAGE SIZE > IMAGE QUALITY SETTINGS option selected.
- **Scroll**: The selector can be used to show portions of the image that are not presently visible on the display when the image is magnified.
- **Multi-Frame Playback**: Rotate the rear command dial to the left when an image is displayed in the full frame to adjust the number of images that are displayed.
- Highlight images with the selector and press MENU/OK to view the highlighted image in its entirety.
- To view additional images in the ninety-frame and one-hundred-frame displays, move the selector up or down.

The DISP/BACK button serves two different purposes:

As a BACK button, it returns the camera to a higher menu or selection level without saving any changes you may have made in the menu sub-level. As a DISPLAY button, it changes the display mode of the currently active view (LCD monitor or viewfinder). It is essential to realize that changing the display mode, does not affect the overall structure of the document. To illustrate, the EVF setting can only be changed when the EVF is turned on and the DISP/BACK button is pressed. This is to say that when you press the DISP/BACK button, you have to look through the EVF, and only then you can see the image in the eye sensor. If not, you will only alter the mode of the display that is currently active on the then LCD monitor. During the shooting mode, the viewfinder as well as the LCD screen can have different display modes at the same time. In playback mode, the EVF and LCD are synchronized into the display mode. In this case, the active display mode (EVF or LCD) doesn't matter since you can switch it by pressing the DISP/BACK button.

Battery Essentials

The Fujifilm X-T5 operates on the FUJIFILM NP-W235 Lithium-Ion Battery. The X-T5 is a lightweight and compact camera for easy carrying. It is armed with modern NP-W235 batteries of 2200 mAh capacity at 16 WH and 7.6V of power. The duration of the battery run varies depending on how you use the camera, but on average, a fully charged battery will last for 500 to 700 shots. **Note**: The X-T5 features an accurate battery indicator with five bars and a percentage display. However, the display's accuracy may depend on using original NP-W235 batteries from Fujifilm. In shooting mode, the percentage display is available only in the INFO display. To activate the INFO display, (repeatedly) press the DISP/BACK button until the INFO display appears on the rear LCD monitor. In playback mode, the percentage indicator is also available in the INFO display, which can be accessed with the DISP/BACK button or by pressing the upper selector key (or moving the focus stick upward) to cycle through two extended image information pages. When the battery indicator shows one remaining red bar, it's almost time to replace/recharge the battery. You can obtain NP-W235 batteries from Fujifilm, or you can use compatible products from third-party vendors. Aftermarket batteries usually don't offer the same quality and performance as the more expensive Fujifilm originals.

FUJIFILM BC-W235 Dual Battery Charger

The FUJIFILM BC-W235 Dual Battery Charger has a dual battery charging function. It provides a quick way to charge Fujifilm batteries. It has a dual design, rather than the usual approach of chargers, that permits users to charge two batteries simultaneously without the need to connect the camera to the wall using a USB cable. This eliminates the mainboard of the camera being damaged by surge and also lessens the tear and wear of the USB port.

Saving Power

- **Auto Power Save:** An option to conserve power has been incorporated into the LCD/EVF displays.
- **ON:** If HIGH PERFORMANCE or STANDARD is selected for POWER MANAGEMENT, the LCD and EVF will transition to a display of standard quality after a predetermined amount of

time passes without any operations being executed. By manipulating the camera controls, the display's fidelity is restored.

- **OFF:** The display quality remains unchanged in the absence of any operations.

USB Charging, Power, and Power banks

Along with spare batteries, the aftermarket also offers external chargers. A high-quality external Power Delivery charger for the new NP-W235 battery is Fujifilm's optional BC-W235 dual charger. This charger requires a USB-C input with at least 15W (better to use 30W) and Power Delivery (PD), and since it doesn't come with a power supply or USB charging cable, you are supposed to use the 15W power supply and the USB-C data/charging cable that came bundled with your X-T5. This means that if you want to charge batteries in the camera and the BC-W235 at the same time, you need a different (or second) power supply and an additional USB-C charging cable with Power Delivery.

Also, instead of external charging batteries, you can charge your batteries directly in the camera by using the USB-C port built into it. Other than USB-C chargers you can buy on your own, you can use a USB-A to USB-C or USB-C to USB-C cable to connect the camera to anything that has a USB output, such as a laptop, phone charger, or a regular power bank. USB chargers and mobile power banks not only charge your X-T5, but they can also power your camera while it is switched on and in use. Fujifilm recommends power banks from Anker, but there are many innovative alternatives from other brands. Just make sure that the power supply or power bank in question offers USB-C Power Delivery and enough wattage to quick-charge your device(s). For example, to quickly charge three batteries (one in your camera and two in an attached dual battery charger) as fast as possible, you need at least 45W (15W + 30W). Please note that even when you power the X-T5 externally, an NP-W235 battery must be inserted into the camera.

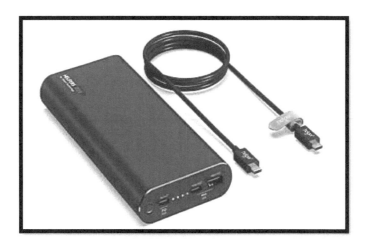

Charge Status

The indicator lamp shows the battery charge status as follows:

- **On:** Battery charging
- **Off:** Charging complete
- **Blinks:** Charging error

Note: The camera is USB-rechargeable. USB charging is compatible with computers that have a USB interface and a manufacturer-approved operating system.

Shooting Specifically for RAW

The X-T5 offers you a choice of uncompressed and compressed RAW files (IMAGE QUALITY SETTING > RAW RECORDING). Lossless compression cuts the size of RAW files roughly in half, so you can store more of them on a memory card or your computer. The compression also helps speed up camera processes. It's important to note that Fujifilm's standard RAW compression is lossless, so there's no difference in image quality between uncompressed and lossless compressed RAWs. The format is widely supported, and RAW converter manufacturers can obtain a free SDK from Fujifilm to support compressed RAW file formats.

Exercise

1. Describe the Exposure Mode and their difference
2. List the focus indicators
3. List the different options for the face/eye detection
4. Discuss OIS and IBIS

CHAPTER 5

SHOOTING ESSENTIALS

How Camera SEE Light - Metering

Metering Modes: There are different methods by which the camera measures exposure.

To do this:

- Press the MENU/OK to show the shooting menu
- Then select PHOTOMETRY, move the selector up or down, and then press MENU/OK.

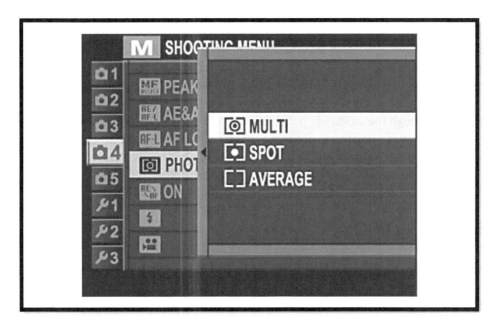

The different options are:

- **Multi**: Using composition, color, and luminance, the camera attempts to determine the optimal exposure by examining the entire scene.
- **Center-Weighted**: While the camera observes the entire scene, it emphasizes the central region.
- **Spot**: The camera meters the lighting in the center of the frame. Ideal for photographs with an extremely bright or dark background.
- **Average**: The exposure is adjusted to the mean value across the entire frame.

ISO Essentials

The quantity of signal amplification applied to an image is determined by ISO. The sensor's native ISO 125 setting serves as the basic calibration for the camera. The signal (or sensor data) is enhanced by one aperture stop (1 EV) at ISO 250 to increase the image's exposure and brightness. The amplification is equivalent to two stops (2 EV) at ISO 500, and so forth. Almost seven stops of additional amplification are applied to the light captured by the sensor at ISO 12800. The correlation between increasing ISO amplification and a decline in image quality is unsurprising, given that noise and artifacts are amplified in addition to the image data itself. In the context of image quality and ISO, a fundamental principle dictates that lower ISO settings yield superior results in terms of quality. Consequently, it is generally advised to maintain the ISO settings at their minimum. Nonetheless, we cannot always shoot at base ISO, particularly in low-light conditions.

Extended ISO

The X-T5 features three additional ISO settings, L (64), H (25600), and H (51200), in addition to the standard ISO settings (ISO 125 to ISO 12800). High (H) signifies that image data is further amplified digitally in these modes. The result of this enormous amplification is a discernible degradation in image quality. ISO 25600 remains functional, particularly when capturing black-and-white JPEGs through the ACROS film simulation. L denotes LOW: When operating in ISO L (64) mode, an ISO 125 RAW is one-stop overexposed. The ISO 64 JPEG file is produced when the JPEG is compressed by one stop and saved during RAW conversion.

Note: Extended ISO settings cannot be used when the electronic shutter (ES) is ON.

Auto Sensitivity (ISO)

Adjustments to the sensitivity (ISO) are implemented automatically via the ISO Auto Setting option under Shooting Menus > Shooting Setting. Minimum Shutter Speed, Maximum Sensitivity (400-12800), and Default Sensitivity (125-12800) are all configurable.

Their default settings are:

- Auto1: ISO 125 sensitivity by default, ISO 800 maximum sensitivity, AUTO minimum shutter speed.
- Auto2: ISO 125 sensitivity by default, ISO 3200 maximum sensitivity, AUTO minimum shutter speed.
- Auto3: ISO 125 sensitivity by default, ISO 12800 maximum sensitivity, AUTO minimum shutter speed.

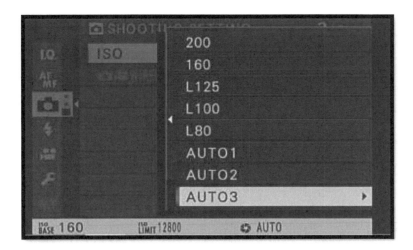

Using manual exposure M

In manual exposure mode, you manually specify all three exposure parameters: aperture, shutter speed, and ISO amplification. For this to work, Auto-ISO must be turned off. Otherwise, ISO would become an exposure variable that the camera would automatically fill. For the live view and live histogram to correctly display the set exposure in manual mode, make sure that SET UP > SCREEN SET-UP > PREVIEW EXP./WB IN MANUAL MODE > PREVIEW EXP./WB is set.

How you can expose it in manual mode

Select and set an aperture and shutter speed that suits your subject and image idea. Aperture controls the depth of field; shutter speed controls the amount of motion blur and camera shake in your exposure. Next, select an ISO value that will yield the desired brightness in your shot. You can (and should) use the live view and live histogram to find a suitable setting. As usual, try not to blow out important highlights. You can check specific parts of your scene by spot-metering them. The exposure scale in the live view screen tells you how much above or below middle gray (zone 5) the spot-metered selection will be exposed. This tool helps you ensure that important parts of your image (such as skin tones or snow) will be exposed exactly like you want them to be. Finally, you may want to readjust or fine-tune the aperture, shutter speed, and ISO according to your metering. Once everything is set, you can take the shot(s).

Auto ISO in Manual Exposure Mode

When Manual mode is combined with Auto-ISO, an additional automatic exposure mode known as "misomatic" is generated. During this mode, the aperture and shutter speed are manually adjusted by the user, while the camera autonomously determines an appropriate ISO setting that corresponds to the exposure as determined by the active metering mode. Auto-ISO should be capable of using the entire ISO bandwidth to function properly in a misomatic setup; therefore, it should be configured with the base ISO 125 of the camera and the maximum available upper limit (ISO 12800). Misomatic provides complete manual control over shutter speed (to prevent motion blur and camera movement) and aperture (to control depth of field). It also provides an exposure compensation dial for adjusting the exposure measured by the camera. It is even more critical to set the MAX SENSITIVITY to its maximum value while the Auto-ISO DEFAULT SENSITIVITY is set to its minimum.

ISO Bracketing

A bracketing amount of ±1/3, ±2/3, or ±1 may be chosen. With each shutter release, the camera will capture an image at the current sensitivity and perform a processing operation to create two additional copies: one with the sensitivity adjusted to the specified level, and the other with the sensitivity decreased accordingly. Each Fuji X camera is capable of ISO bracketing. One exposure is captured in this mode, and the camera generates three output files at various ISO settings. As an example, if the ISO of the camera is set to 400 and the ISO bracketing is established at +/ -1 EV, the initial JPG image of the set of three will be captured at ISO 400, the second at ISO 800, and the third at ISO 200.

White Balance (WB)

The built-in RAW converter of all the X-series cameras offers the users the option to control the white balance and JPEG parameters either before or after the image is taken. It is the process of compressing the image files obtained from the camera, giving full control of their quality.

The X-T5 provides the following options for manually adjusting the white balance: A variety of white balance profiles are tailored to common circumstances, including tungsten light (Incandescent), cloudy skies (Shade), and sunny weather (Fine). A custom white balance is designed to measure a neutral or white surface, such as a wall, in the presence of ambient light. By doing so, the white balance of the surface can be adjusted by the camera to render it neutral. Three distinct positions are available on the X-T5 for custom WB settings. Additionally, the AUTO white balance of the camera can be adjusted to emphasize either the ambiance of a scene (AUTO AMBIENCE PRIORITY) or a neutral outcome (AUTO WHITE PRIORITY). For natural colors, choose a white balance option that matches the light source.

The different options are:

- **AUTO WHITE PRIORITY:** The white balance is automatically corrected. Go for whiter whites in incandescent scenes and more natural tones in daylight.
- **AUTO:** With white balance the camera automatically does the adjustment.

- **AUTO AMBIENCE PRIORITY:** The white balance is made automatically. For incandescent bulbs, go with the warmer whites in the scenes.
- **CUSTOM 1, 2 and 3:** Incur a value of white balance.
- **COLOR TEMPERATURE**: Choose a color temperature.
- **DAYLIGHT:** For subjects in the direct solar rays.
- **SHADE:** For plants in the shadow of the trees.
- **FLUORESCENT LIGHT-1:** Use compact fluorescent lights in the warehouse under "daylight" mode.
- **FLUORESCENT LIGHT-2:** Use light fixtures with warm white fluorescent tubes under them.
- **FLUORESCENT LIGHT-3:** Employ the use of "cool white" fluorescent lamps under them.
- **SUBTLE INCREMENTAL CHOICES:** make your choices subtle and incremental.
- **UNDERWATER** is a special kind of filtration that eliminates the blue cast of the water that is caused by underwater lighting.

Custom white balance can be achieved with minimal effort

This feature is accessible before capturing an image, as it measures the white balance of the scene itself. By using custom white balance, one can adjust the white balance of the camera to a specific element of the scene neutral in the resulting photograph

To do this:

Go to IMAGE QUALITY SETTING > WHITE BALANCE > CUSTOM. The X-T5 supports the setting and saving of three distinct custom white balance parameters (CUSTOM 1–3). Directing the camera in the direction of a neutral reference surface, such as a grey card or a white wall. Ensure the surface is sufficiently expansive to fully cover the white balance metering frame in the viewfinder. If necessary, move closer to your subject or zoom in. Press the shutter button to its maximum position and configure the white balance to your liking. The real-time display will adjust in response and replicate the modified hue temperature. Confirm your satisfaction with the outcome by clicking the OK button.

Changing color tints with WB Shift

WB shift enables the introduction (or correction) of a color tint in any shot. In addition, with any white balance setting, the color hint can be modified before or after capturing an image or through the built-in RAW converter. A different white balance shift can be configured for each of the white balance options offered by the camera, including Auto, Custom white balance setting, Kelvin, and WB presets. To do this, adjust the values along the Y-axis, which transitions from yellow to blue, and the X-axis, which spans from green to red, respectively, on the display that appears automatically upon selecting a white balance option. It is advisable to use a neutral setting to prevent any potential confusion. Note that each white balance option has its white balance shift setting; therefore, the camera can temporarily retain a maximum of twelve white balance shift settings. This renders it excessively simple to overlook a previously set correction; thus, it is better to use a white balance shift exclusively during RAW conversion.

Autofocus Options-AF Modes

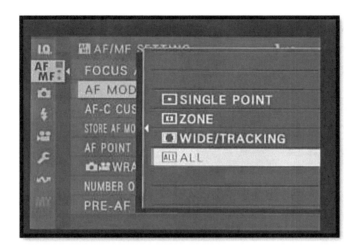

Menus for Shooting > AF/MF Setting > AF Mode. The options are:

- **Single Point**: Use a single point when in AF-S Focus mode to achieve precise, critical focus.
- **Zone**: The subject is automatically focused on by the camera within the designated focus zone. Multiple focus points are used in the focus zones, which facilitates the concentration on moving subjects.
- **Wide**: The camera automatically focuses on subjects with high contrast.
- **All**: This enables you to cycle through the Single Point, Zone, and Wide AF modes using the Rear Command dial while in the focus point selection display.

AF-C Custom Settings

Choose AF-C CUSTOM SETTINGS from the AF/MF SETTINGS menu, and then select one of the available parameter sets:

- **SET 1:** MULTI PURPOSE is the general AF-C setting and the default value. This option is good in circumstances where a precise comprehension of how a particular customized setting might enhance the AF-C's performance is lacking. The parameter configurations consist of TS 2, STS 0, and ZAS AUTO.

- **SET 2:** IGNORE OBSTACLES & CONTINUE TO TRACK SUBJECT maintains the subject's focus even when it has been temporarily obscured by obstacles or has left the frame. Implementing this feature can prove advantageous in the context of camera tracking, as it guarantees the target remains in focus even when it becomes momentarily obscured by obstructions such as trees, people, or other barriers that obstruct the line of sight to the target. The values of its parameters are TS 3, STS 0, and ZAS CENTRE.
- **SET 3:** FOR ACCELERATING/DECELERATING SUBJECT is typical racetrack mode. It considers the changing relative speed of subjects approaching the camera. This mode can be handy when confronted with targets that accelerate or decelerate rapidly, particularly when used in conjunction with XF lenses that have high-speed linear autofocus motors. The parameter configurations consist of TS 2, STS 2, and ZAS AUTO.
- **SET 4:** FOR SUDDENLY APPEARING SUBJECT enables the camera to focus instantaneously on a subject that enters the focusing area, giving precedence to the closest object. It is optimal for subjects that enter the focusing frame abruptly. The parameter configurations consist of TS 0, STS 1, and ZAS FRONT.
- **SET 5:** FOR ACCELERATING/DECELERATING MOVING SUBJECTS is suitable for subjects that are moving at varying speeds in different directions, coming in and out of the focusing area. It is optimized for shooting field sports like soccer or tennis. Of course, this also applies to playing with kids or dogs. Its parameter settings are TS 3, STS 2, and ZAS AUTO.
- **SET 6:** CUSTOM: It customizes the three AF-C subject-tracking parameters (TS), STS (SPEED TRACKING SENSITIVITY), and ZAZ (ZONE AREA SWITCHING) with the user-specified value. By using this preset, one can manually generate optimized parameters that cater to the particular movement attributes of the subject.

Flash Essentials

In flash photography, a double exposure is captured. Ambient light and flashlight are the two elements that comprise the illumination in every flash photograph. The ambient light component is measured in the same manner as a standard exposure. The scene is being metered by the camera using one of several methods: spot, average, multi-exposure, or center-weighted. In contrast, the auto exposure mode (P, A, or S) selects appropriate exposure parameters automatically in response to your adjustments on the exposure compensation dial. Additionally, the exposure of the ambient light component can be adjusted manually in mode M. In essence, exposing the ambient light component is identical to exposing a scene in the absence of a flash. The flash-light component may be metered and adjusted automatically by the camera to correspond with the overall exposure. To achieve this objective, the camera uses a metering system known as TT. TTL is the abbreviation for "through the lens." It indicates that the flashlight penetrates the camera via the lens before the image sensor receives a reading.

This is achieved through the emission of a weakened pre-flash, which serves only the purpose of metering. The intensity of the automatic flash-light component can be adjusted via the FLASH FUNCTION SETTING page or by connecting external Fujifilm TTL flash units, such as the EF-X500, to the flash unit directly. It is important to acknowledge that although the live view and live histogram offer a sneak peek of the ambient-light component, they do not account for the flash-light component that will be incorporated into the final image. In addition to Fujifilm-branded or Fujifilm-compatible TTL flash units, generic third-party flash units may also be used. When generic third-party flash units are used, TTL flash metering is no longer accessible; therefore, the power output of the flash must be adjusted manually. Additionally, automatic flash units with built-in light sensors that measure and regulate the flash output autonomously and separate from the camera are also available.

Understanding flash modes

You can select from a variety of flash modes supported by the TTL flash logic on your X-T5 via the Quick menu or the FLASH SETTING > FLASH FUNCTION SETTING.

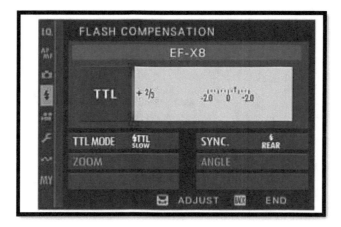

The TTL FLASH AUTO function is exclusive to the auto exposure mode P. If the camera determines that an available flash unit is required, it will activate automatically. TTL STANDARD discharges an active flash unit at all times. This configuration is accessible across all four modes of exposure (P, A, S, and M). The weakest shutter speed available in modes P and A (where the autoexposure of the camera governs the shutter speed) is 1/60 second; therefore, areas of the scene where the flashlight component cannot illuminate may be underexposed. TTL SLOW SYNC. Functions similarly to conventional TTL, but permits shutter velocities below 1/60 second to more effectively capture the ambient light component. When the lighting is poor but you still wish to capture a significant portion of the background, this can be useful. This setting is exclusive to modes P and A of exposure. Nevertheless, when used in conjunction with AUTO-ISO, this mode will only decelerate by 1/60 second if the AE-determined shutter speed is slower than the MIN. SHUTTER SPEED setting and AUTO-ISO have reached the ISO ceiling set with MAX. SENSITIVITY. Therefore, it is not advisable to use AUTO-ISO in conjunction with TTL SLOW Sync light photography. Similar to TTL SLOW Sync, MANUAL FLASH enables the user to specify the light flash emission intensity manually. This configuration is accessible across all four modes of exposure (P, A, S, and M).

OFF ensures that no light is discharged, despite the flash being connected to the camera and powered on. Also available on the light FUNCTION SETTING page is the option to specify whether the light should be directed at the rear (2nd CURTAIN) or front (1st CURTAIN). This option is applicable when photographing moving subjects with slow shutter speeds and is accessible in all flash modes. Given that flash photography operates on the principle of double exposure, the timing of the flash discharge during an extended ambient light exposure is significant. In the case of high-end flashguns such as the EF-X500, an additional setting known as FP (Focal Plane) is also available. High-speed synchronization (HSS) is implemented by Fuji and permits the flash to be discharged at any mechanical shutter speed of up to 1/8000 second.

Controlling the ambient-light component

When metering a scene with the X-T5, it becomes evident that the activation or deactivation of the flash function makes no difference. Constantly, the metering result will be identical. In other words, the camera consistently measures the ambient light component regardless of the presence or absence of a flash. Should you opt to use a flash, the flash-light component will be seamlessly incorporated into the ambient-light component. This is significant because it reassures us that there is no need to be concerned about camera voodoo that may or may not affect the ambient light metering when a flash is activated. Conversely, it can be guaranteed that the metering of the camera will consistently produce reliable outcomes. Consequently, achieving an equilibrium between the two light components becomes your responsibility. For instance, to accommodate more flashlights in the composite exposure, we may need to reduce the ambient light component. The exposure of the ambient-light component can be modified manually (ISO, aperture, shutter speed), through the use of the exposure compensation dial, or by adjusting the exposure compensation dial to the desired level. In the pursuit of achieving balanced outcomes, a greater flash-light component will be incorporated into the TTL flash metering in response to reduced ambient light. Altering the exposure compensation dial exclusively impacts the exposure of the ambient light component of the photo, without any discernible impact on the flash component.

To use the live view and live histogram to manipulate the ambient-light component in manual mode M, ensure that the exposure preview is enabled in manual mode by navigating to SETUP > SCREEN SET-UP > PREVIEW EXP./WB IN MANUAL MODE > PREVIEW EXP./WB. When working in a studio environment, it is a common practice to reduce the influence of ambient light and strictly use a flashlight to illumine the subject. When this is the case, it is better to use a base ISO of 125, smaller aperture settings (larger aperture numbers), and a quick shutter speed. 1/250 second is the maximum official flash synchronization speed of the X-T5. Occasionally, even at base ISO, the quickest available flash sync speed will overexpose the ambient light component. Although one could reduce the aperture, doing so could potentially defeat the purpose of using a shallow depth of field to create a pleasing separation between the subject and the background. When this occurs, it is okay to affix a neutral density filter to the lens to reduce by three to six stops the amount of light that reaches the sensor. Alternatively, you may use a high-speed sync (HSS) flash that is Fuji-compatible.

Controlling the flash-light component

One may adjust the brightness or darkness of the flash-light component of an image by using a bias function on the camera's TTL flash system:

To bias the flash-light component of an image, one may modify the flash exposure compensation via the FLASH SETTING > FLASH FUNCTION SETTING page on the camera with several external TTL flash units. Depending on the specific flash unit being used, combining the in-camera flash compensation with an additional compensation preset on the flash unit may result in the addition of both corrections. Frequently, nicer-looking results can be obtained by reflecting the flash off the ceiling, as this mitigates the intensity of the flashlight. More power is required to bounce the flashlight, so you may require a stronger flash. Additionally, light that is refracted by bouncing off a colored surface will be tinted proportionately. To alter the color temperature or impart a tint to a flashlight, colored gel filters may be joined close to the reflector. In general, the color temperature of unfiltered flashlights is equivalent to that of natural daylight. The range of your flash unit is contingent upon the aperture, and ISO, among other settings. While the camera adjusts the light intensity of the flash automatically in TTL mode, many flash units also offer the option to operate manually. You can adjust the power output of the flash. Changing the shutter speed in manual mode M does not affect the luminosity of the torch component of the image as long as the sync speed remains at or below the official maximum of 1/250 second. Therefore, modifying the shutter speed serves as a rapid method to alter the exposure of the ambient light component while preserving the precision of your manually balanced flash-light setup. Bear in mind that the use of an on-camera hot-shoe flash may be hindered by undesirable shadows caused by lens hoods and large lenses that obstruct portions of the flashlight. Removing the lens hood or using an off-camera light is preferable.

Front-curtain vs. rear-curtain flash synchronization

Flash photographs are composed of two exposures—flashlight and ambient light—merged. When capturing ambient light with a slow shutter speed, the timing of the flash's (considerably faster) discharge becomes an issue. Typically, the flash is initiated when the shutter opens its FRONT (or 1st) curtain to commence an exposure. Nevertheless, if the REAR (or 2nd) curtain is chosen, the flash discharges as the rear shutter curtain retracts towards the conclusion of the exposure. Moving objects inherently undergo positional changes throughout the exposure of a photograph. By coordinating the flash with the rear curtain, it is possible to freeze moving objects after the exposure, rather than at the start. Consequently, the moving object frequently appears more natural in the resulting image. **Note:** The rear-curtain model removes the false impression that a car for example is reversing and provides a more natural appearance. This further demonstrates the use of flash photographs as double exposures. The slow shutter speed renders the moving vehicle a hazy trail of light, whereas the rapid flash freezes portions of it in an instant.

Red-eye removal

The red-eye effect can occur when the flash and the subject are nearly aligned along the same optical axis. This occurs frequently with hot-shoe flashes and causes an undesirable crimson reflection in the eyes. By selecting FLASH SETTING > RED EYE REMOVAL followed by the FLASH button, the camera will initiate a pre-flash just before each picture. This pre-flash compels the subject's pupils to constrict, thereby effectively reducing or removing the red-eye effect.

Using TTL-Lock

AE-Lock is analogous to TTL-Lock. TTL-Lock controls the exposure of the flash-light component, whereas AE-Lock controls the exposure of the ambient light component. Before using TTL-Lock, it must be assigned to one of the Fn controls on your camera. To accomplish this, hold down the DISP/BACK key until the Fn configuration screen loads.

TTL-Lock can operate in two distinct ways:

Cancel and maintain the exposure of the most recent flash exposure by activating the TTL-Lock function (access via FLASH SETTINGS > TTL-LOCK MODE > LOCK WITH LAST FLASH). Lock the metered result immediately after setting the TTL-Lock button and metering the flash exposure with a metering flash (FLASH SETTING > TTL-LOCK MODE > LOCK WITH METERING FLASH). When you want to capture multiple images of the same scene while maintaining a consistent flash output throughout the series, TTL-Lock is a useful feature. A customized procedure entails activating the LOCK WITH LAST FLASH function, subsequently capturing several test photos of the scene, and lastly adjusting the flash exposure compensation until the outcome is satisfactory. While continuing to capture additional images of the scene, lock and sustain this "perfect" flash exposure by pressing TTL-Lock. TTL-Lock permits increased frame rates during burst mode as well. You will likely prefer the LOCK WITH METERING FLASH configuration in this circumstance. After metering the scene and storing the calculated flash exposure, press TTL-Lock. The frame rate will increase as you proceed to capture images in burst mode, as the camera will not be required to generate and analyze a new metering flare before each frame.

Exercise

1. List the Metering Mode
2. Describe the manual exposure mode
3. **What is flash photography**

CHAPTER 6

FILMS, SIMS, FILTERS, CURVES, COLOR CHROME AND TONING

Film Simulation

There are over 19 film simulations on the X-T5 as discussed earlier. Let's look at some of them

Classic Chrome: Classic Chrome is a film simulation that is meant to look like documentary magazines from the 20th century. It has low saturation and hard tonal gradation in the shadows; hence it's great for documentary photography.

Astia/Soft: This film simulation mode focuses on showing skin tones softly and accurately, while also showing clear blue skies and greenery.

Velvia/Vivid: This film mode gives you colors that are richer and have more contrast than provia/standard. This is the mode that nature photographers love to use. It has one primary color that is more deeply saturated.

Provia/Standard: This film simulation setting works well with all kinds of subjects because it reproduces colors evenly. When you turn on a Fujifilm camera for the first time and set it up, the Provia profile is what you see from the color profile. It has natural colors and a modest amount of contrast.

Eterna/Cinema: This mode of film emulation reduces saturation to prevent any one color from dominating another. To prevent clipping and replicate a cinematic appearance, it produces highlights with exceptionally soft tonal gradation and deep shadows.

Acros: This film simulation mode gives you deep shadow details and great sharpness. At high ISOs, it still adds grain and recreates the beautiful textured feel of black and white film.

Nostalgic Negative: This effect is meant to make a picture look like it's from an old photo album. It produces pictures with rich colors in the shadows and a gentle tone in the highlights and mid-tone.

Classic Negative: This simulation mode provides tonal gradation with high contrast. It reduces saturation while adjusting the tones of highlights and shadows to add definition and depth to colors.

Pro Negative Standard and Hi

The pro-Neg. standard mode has a softer look that isn't too different from Astia. It focuses on natural skin tones and has less contrast so that changes between colors are smoother. The Hi profile is stronger placing greater emphasis on contrast. If you are attempting to highlight shadows but are hindered by overcast lighting conditions, this is a suitable option.

Eterna Bleach Bypass

Bleach Bypass is a new form of Eterna. This mode makes the film look like it was made using the bleach bypass method, which doesn't get rid of the silver crystals. It gives the picture a dull look with few dark details and strong contrast.

Sepia

The Sepia profile takes the basic Monochrome look and gives it a brownish tint.

Film Recipes – Combining Sims and Settings

Users of Fujifilm X-series can load combinations of settings into their cameras that allow shooting in a variety of styles. The settings include a choice of built-in film simulation mode, the white balance, and adjustments to the tone curve, sharpness, and saturation. These saved setting combinations are known as film recipes. Their big advantage over traditional raw shooting is that the images can be used directly from the camera with no further editing in expensive software.

Let's look at some top Fujifilm Film Recipe Film

Kodak Portra 400 v2

Kodak Portra 400 v2 is a Recipe that produces acceptable images at any daylight hour. It is great for golden hour, which is to say the time near sunrise and sunset. You could make this your go-to C1 All-the-time recipe, but when the sun is low to the horizon, this should be the one you're capturing with.

C3 — Kodak Ultramax 400

For a rainy day, the Kodak Ultramax 400 is a good choice. It is a reliable recipe; however, it is not only appropriate for rainy moments but also for the golden hours, midday, shade, indoors, nighttime, and so on

Timeless Negative - Indoor

As regards indoor photography using natural light, the Timeless Negative Recipe is better (however, any of the Recipes below this could work as well). Timeless Negative goes along with different situations and gives high-quality results, suitable for natural light indoor pictures.

Superia Xtra 400 — Nighttime

The Superia Xtra 400 is a great Recipe for all the C1-C4 issues; also it's a multipurpose one and could be your default choice for any situation.

Vintage Bronze — Wildcard

The Vintage Bronze which produces vintage analog-like results in a wide variety of situations either indoors or in daylight is another film recipe. It was derived from the Eterna Bleach Bypass film sim.

Ilford FP4 Plus 125 — B&W

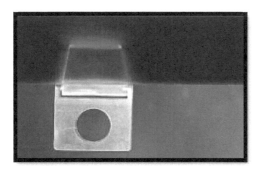

When we talk about FP4 plus 125, the only black-and-white Recipe that is specifically designed to be used on X-Trans V cameras, it's a very good Recipe! However, X-Trans IV B&W Recipes incorporate X-Trans V camera lines, too. This is suitable for those who want a deep, emotional, and thought-provoking experience.

Advanced Filter

A collection of creative effect filters comprised of Advanced Filters. You may argue that gimmicks are unnecessary, but they can be entertaining to manipulate. In SHOOTING SETTING > DRIVE SETTING > ADV. FILTER SETTING, rotate the DRIVE dial to the ADV. position to access the filters. From there, choose one of thirteen available filter options. Advanced Filters not only generates a JPEG or HEIF file showcasing the applied effect but also preserves a RAW file for future use in producing a "regular" image devoid of elaborate filter effects. This can be accomplished with either the integrated RAW converter or an external RAW converter such as Lightroom. Nevertheless, there are two considerations to bear in mind:

Choose from the following filters:

TOY CAMERA: Go for a retro camera look

MINIATURE: At the top and bottom of the picture, a diorama-like effect is created by the blurring of the images.

POP COLOR: Use dark backgrounds and bright colors for high-contrast images.

HIGH-KEY: Create bright, low-contrast images.

LOW-KEY: Create uniformly dark tones with a few areas of emphasized highlights.

DYNAMIC TONE: Dynamic tone expression is used for a fantasy effect.

SOFT FOCUS: Create a look that is evenly soft throughout the whole image.

PARTIAL COLOR (RED): Areas of the image that are the selected color are recorded in red color. All other areas of the image are recorded in black-and-white.

PARTIAL COLOR (ORANGE)

PARTIAL COLOR (YELLOW)

PARTIAL COLOR (GREEN)

PARTIAL COLOR (BLUE)

PARTIAL COLOR (PURPLE)

Photo (Still) Menu Setting

Here you can choose a lot of things, but the most important are the styling options of your image and how it will look in the end. Let us look at some of these.

IMAGE QUALITY SETTING (Still Photography):

1/4

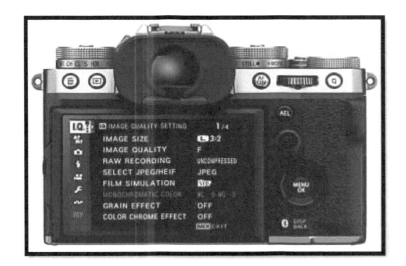

2/4

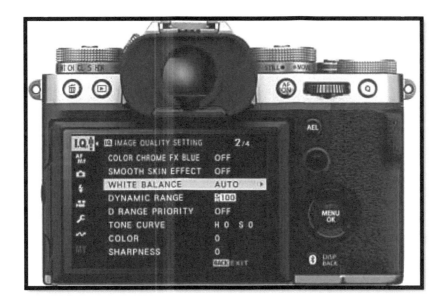

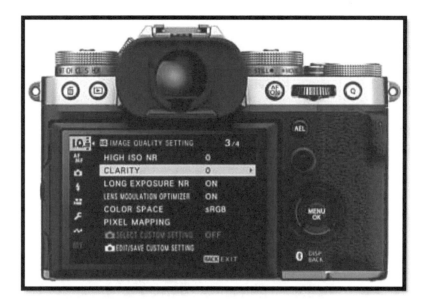

You can change the settings for image quality when taking still pictures. To see the settings for picture quality, press MENU/OK on the camera's screen and choose (IMAGE QUALITY SETTING)

Note: The choices you have depend on the shot mode you choose.

IMAGE SIZE

You can choose what size and aspect ratio to take still images at. You can choose from three sizes: large, medium, and small. Large is the full sensor size, so every pixel will be recorded without downsizing. Medium is half that size, and small is half of medium, or 25 times the size of large.

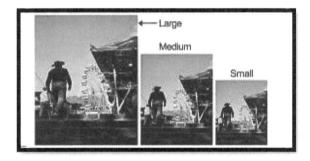

The table below shows the image size and aspect ratio.

Option	Image size	Option	Image size
L 3:2	7728 × 5152	L 4:3	6864 × 5152
L 16:9	7728 × 4344	L 5:4	6432 × 5152
L 1:1	5152 × 5152		

Option	Image size	Option	Image size
M 3:2	5472 × 3648	M 4:3	4864 × 3648
M 16:9	5472 × 3080	M 5:4	4560 × 3648
M 1:1	3648 × 3648		

Option	Image size	Option	Image size
S 3:2	3888 × 2592	S 4:3	3456 × 2592
S 16:9	3888 × 2184	S 5:4	3264 × 2592
S 1:1	2592 × 2592		

An example of the image ratio is shown below

IMAGE QUALITY

This option lets you choose a file type and a compression ratio. The options are:

- FINE: Images with better quality use low compression ratios.
- NORMAL: More pictures can be saved by using higher compression ratios.
- FINE+RAW: You can record both RAW and high-quality JPEG or HEIF photos.
- NEW + RAW: You can record both RAW and regular JPEG or HEIF photos.
- RAW: Only record RAW pictures.

RAW RECORDING

With this option, you can choose whether to compress the size of RAW files. The options are:

- **UNCOMPRESSED:** RAW files are uncompressed.
- **LOSSLESS COMPRESSED:** The reversible algorithm is the one that shrinks the RAW files without losing any data from images.
- **COMPRESSED:** A "lossy" algorithm is used to compress RAW images in a way that can't be uncompressed, thus removing the possibility of recovering the original quality of an image. Files are about 25% to 35% reduced in size when compressed but the quality is the same as when they were not compressed.

SELECT JPEG/HEIF

Use to choose whether to take pictures in JPEG or HEIF.

- **JPEG:** Pictures are saved in the JPEG format, which is widely used.
- **HEIF:** Pictures are saved in HEIF, a file that compresses well but doesn't give you many ways to view or share them.

FILM SIMULATION: This option simulates the effect of different types of film, like black-and-white (with or without color filters). Pick a palette that fits your theme and your creative goals.

MONOCHROMATIC COLOR

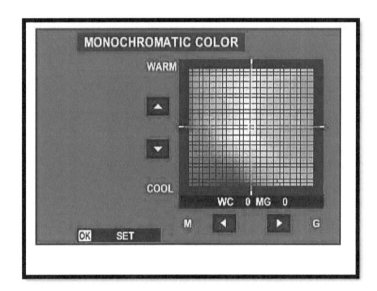

Color cast the ACROS and MONOCHROME film models more red or blue. This is also known as adding a warm or cool tint. The WARM–COOL and G (Green)–M (Magenta) axes can be used to change the color.

- **GRAIN EFFECT:** It adds the film grain effect to an image
- **ROUGHNESS:** It shows are rough an image looks. Can either be strong for a rougher grain, weak for a smoother grain, or off to turn off the effect.
- **COLOR CHROME EFFECT:** This option makes more tones available for showing colors like reds, yellows, and greens that are prone to be very saturated.
- **COLOR CHROME FX BLUE:** It adds more tones to the palette that can be used to create blues.
- **SMOOTH SKIN EFFECT:** It makes skin smooth.
- **WHITE BALANCE:** Pick a white balance setting that fits the light source for natural colors.

The options are:

- AUTO: The white balance is changed on its own.
- AUTO AMBIENCE PRIORITY: The white balance is changed by itself. When incandescent lights are used, choose warmer whites for scenes.
- CUSTOM 1, 2, and 3: Find a white balance number.
- COLOR TEMPERATURE: It's up to you to pick a color temperature.
- DAYLIGHT: For things that are in full sunlight.
- SHADE: For things that are in the shade.
- FLUORESCENT LIGHT-1: Put this light under "daylight" fluorescent lights.
- FLUORESCENT LIGHT-2: Put this light under "warm white" fluorescent lights.
- FLUORESCENT LIGHT-3: Put this light under "cool white" fluorescent lights.
- INCANDESCENT Use under incandescent lighting.
- UNDERWATER cuts down on the blue cast that undersea lighting usually has.

DYNAMIC RANGE

This option changes the dynamic range. Wide dynamic ranges keep details from being lost in the highlights, so scenes with a lot of contrast or backlighting look more realistic.

D RANGE PRIORITY

When taking pictures of scenes with a lot of contrast, reduce the loss of detail in the highlights and shadows to get results that look more natural. The options are:

- Auto to change the contrast automatically based on the lighting.
- Strong, to adjust dynamic range with lots of contrast.
- Weak for scenes with a modest amount of contrast, and off to turn off contrast reduction.

TONE CURVE

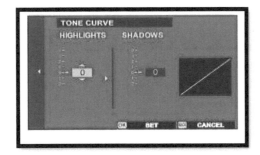

Using a tone curve as a guide, change how highlights or shadows look by making them sharper or softer. To make shadows and highlights sharper, set the value higher. To make them softer, set the value lower.

- HIGHLIGHTS: -2 to +4
- SHADOWS: -2 to +4

COLOR

It changes the amount of color. −4 −3 −2 −1 0 +1 +2 +3 +4

SHARPNESS

It makes the outlines sharper or weaker.

HIGH ISO NR

Lessen the noise in photos that were taken with high sensitivity. Pick values that are higher to get rid of noise and make outlines smooth, and values that are lower to keep outlines clear.

CLARITY

Boost the definition while making as few changes as possible to the tones in the highlights and shadows. If you want more clarity, choose higher values. If you want a softer effect, choose lower values.

LONG EXPOSURE NR

- To get rid of mottling caused by long shots, choose ON.
- It can be ON or OFF.

Note: When ON is chosen, save times are longer because more work is needed.

LENS MODULATION OPTIMIZER

If you choose "ON," the definition will be better because the lens will correct for distortion and the slight loss of focus around the edges.

COLOR SPACE

Pick the range of colors that can be used for color reproduction.

- **SRGB:** This color scheme is usually a good idea.
- **Adobe RGB:** For commercial for business.

PIXEL MAPPING

Use this option if you see bright spots in your photos.

SELECT CUSTOM SETTING: The settings you saved to custom settings banks 1 through 7 (CUSTOM 1 through CUSTOM 7) by pressing EDIT and then SAVE CUSTOM SETTING.

EDIT/SAVE CUSTOM SETTING

You can change options and save them to a bank of custom settings. IMAGE QUALITY SETTING > SELECT CUSTOM SETTING lets you get back to the settings that you have saved.

Saving Custom Settings

- Go to IMAGE QUALITY SETTING > EDIT/SAVE CUSTOM SETTING in the shooting menu and press MENU/OK.
- Choose a bank where the new settings will go (CREATE NEW C1 through C7) and press MENU/OK. There will be a confirmation message box.
- Click on OK and then press MENU/OK. The chosen bank will store the current camera settings.

Editing Custom Settings

Change custom settings banks that are already there.
1: Go to the shot menu and press MENU/OK. Then, choose IMAGE QUALITY SETTING > EDIT/SAVE CUSTOM SETTING.

2: Select the desired settings bank you want and press MENU/OK.
3: Click on EDIT/CHECK and then press MENU/OK.

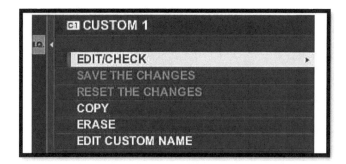

85

4 The camera will show you a list of shooting menu items. Pick out the one you want to change and press MENU/OK. Change the item that was chosen as needed.

5 To save your changes and go back to the shooting menu list, press MENU/OK.

AUTO UPDATE CUSTOM SETTING

You can choose whether saved changes to custom settings should be applied immediately.

- **ENABLE:** When you make changes to custom settings banks CUSTOM 1 through CUSTOM 7, they are immediately applied.
- **DISABLE:** The changes won't take effect right away. Any changes that are made to custom settings have to be done manually.

MOUNT ADAPTOR SETTING

Change the settings for lenses that are connected with a mount adapter. Setting for six lenses (LENS 1 through LENS 6) can be saved in the camera.

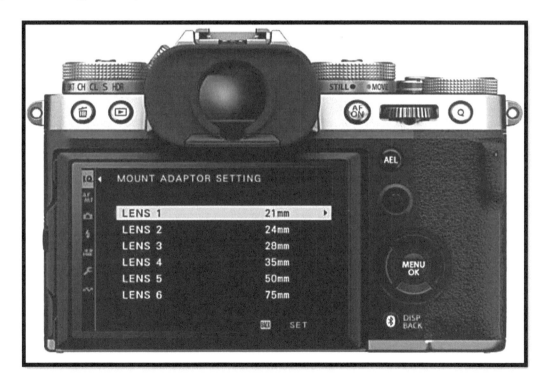

Note: The image can be CORRECTED FROM DISTORTION, COLOR SHADING, and PERIPHERAL ILLUMINATION when you attach your lenses to an M mount adapter.

When the mount adapter is being used, the focal length of the lens has to be set in the mount adapter setting. This is the only time you need to do this, and knowing the focal length of the lens will help your camera make other settings work better. Like the lens modulation optimizer, you can set other types of distortion control here in the amount adapter setting menu. You can do this by hand and change things like distortion, vignetting (also called "barrel" or "pin cushion"), and peripheral light correction.

Exercise

1. List 5 major film simulation
2. Describe the advance filter
3. List the options in the photo (still) menu setting

CHAPTER 7

DRIVE MODES

HDR

HDR is the technique of merging several images that are captured at different exposure levels of a scene into one enhanced and realistic image. Although HDR usually demands at least two separate exposures of a scene, the film is made of five, seven, or even nine distinct exposures with a common stop or one EV (exposure value) between them.

The following method will enable you to generate nine distinct exposures of a single scene efficiently:

Put the camera on a tripod or any similar device. Arrange the self-timer for two seconds or connect a remote shutter release to prevent camera shake. Adjust the camera to aperture priority A, choose BKT via the DRIVE dial, and check that the AE BKT option is enabled in the following menu: SHOOTING SETTING > DRIVE SETTING > BKT SETTING > BKT SELECT.

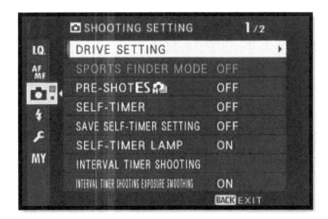

- Select a low ISO value, such as the default ISO 125. Avoid using extended ISO L
- Deactivate any DR expansion by configuring DR-P to OFF and the dynamic range to 100%.
- Apply manual focus and choose an aperture that is appropriate for the scene and photograph. Additionally, you may use adapted manual focus lenses if necessary.
- Set AE BKT (auto exposure bracketing) with a variation of ±1 EV across nine frames (FRAMES STEP SETTING > SHOOTING SETTING > DRIVE SETTING > BKT SETTING > AE BKT).
- Choose AVERAGE exposure metering.

Now that the camera has been set for HDR, the actual images can be captured:

Manually focus the scene, adjust the exposure compensation dial to neutral (0), and execute the shutter release action. Use either the self-timer or remote shutter activation. In the next nine frames, the camera will capture an interval of +4 EV to -4 EV. This process generates nine distinct exposures, which can subsequently be combined utilizing the HDR software of preference. An additional 4 EVs will be added to the dynamic range of the resultant image.

HDR: the manual way

One can proficiently capture handheld HDR images with the X-T5's ISO-fewer sensors by combining two or three RAW files with distinct exposures into a single HDR-DNG file using Lightroom or Adobe Camera RAW. **To begin, it is important to set the camera:**

- Following the activation of aperture priority A on the X-T5, ensure that AE BKT is configured in SHOOTING SETTING > DRIVE SETTING > BKT SETTING > BKT SELECT and select BKT on the DRIVE dial.
- Arrange the ISO setting to a low value, like ISO 125. Avoid using extended ISO L.
- Ensure that the dynamic range is configured to DR100% and that the DR-P option is deactivated.
- Pre-select an appropriate aperture.
- Configure AE BKT in the SHOOTING SETTING > DRIVE SETTING > BKT SETTING > AE BKT > FRAME/STEP SETTING menu with a variation of +3 FRAMES and a 2 STEP.
- Additionally, the "JPEG settings for RAW shooters" configuration (film simulation ETERNA, TONE CURVE (SHADOWS) −2, and TONE CURVE (HIGHLIGHTS) −2) may be of interest. This may assist you in determining the optimal exposure for the scene's highlights and framing.

Let's now capture HDR images:

Expose to the highlights! Frame your scene using the live view and live histogram, and then adjust the exposure compensation dial until the desired highlights are not blown out. To capture the image, maintain focus and press the shutter button without recomposing the scene in the process. Maintain complete control of the camera as it rapidly fires three AE bracketing photos (each with a unique exposure) in succession. Import the RAW files containing the three bracketed images into a single HDR-DNG file using the HDR function in Lightroom or Adobe Camera RAW. Lightroom can subsequently analyze the HDR-DNG file in the same manner as any other RAW file. By merging three exposures with a 2 EV difference between each, the dynamic range of the image as a whole is significantly increased.

Due to the rapid succession of photos captured at maximum continuous drive speed, the resultant DNG composite image exhibits minimal to negligible motion blur. Even (slowly) moving subjects can be captured using this method, given that the HDR merge tool in Lightroom incorporates automatic ghosting. The highlights are precisely exposed to the darkest of the three images, while the remaining two exposures contain 2 EV and 4 EV less noise, respectively. Due to the minimal sensor read noise produced by our ISO-less sensor, it is effortless to increase the brightness of the three RAWs by an additional 3 EV without significantly degrading the image quality. This provides an astounding 7 EV of additional dynamic range, which should be sufficient to surmount virtually any challenge you may face in the realm of photography about dynamic range. Even better, this method can be applied to handheld images; simply ensure that the brightest image's shutter speed is sufficient to prevent camera shake-induced blur.

Using the built-in HDR function

The built-in HDR function of the X-T5 is concealed within the DRIVE dial. Set the DRIVE dial to HDR and choose one of the five HDR modes available in SHOOTING SETTING > DRIVE SETTING > HDR MODE—AUTO, 200%, 400%, 800%, or 800%+—to activate it. The HDR function of Fujifilm is conceptually very similar to its long-standing DR function: By exposing images darker than what is indicated by the EXIF data, live view, and camera settings, it increases the dynamic range of the highlights. HDR utilizes three frames as opposed to DR's one: DR operates with a single shot, while HDR employs three frames: one "master frame" exposed with the specified and indicated parameters, and two additional frames exposed at a lower intensity than the master frame. When in HDR mode, the camera combines three frames with distinct exposures to generate a composite JPEG, HEIF, or TIFF file that possesses an increased dynamic range of highlights. Additionally, a container-style RAW file is created and saved, which contains the RAW data of the three images with varying exposures. HDR RAW files are consequently approximately three times the size of standard single-shot RAW files.

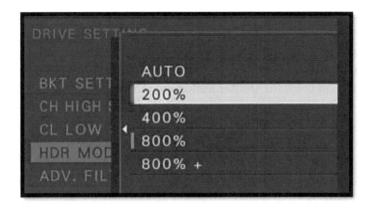

HDR AUTO determines the appropriate values of 200%, 400%, or 800% contrast based on the live view scene's contrast range. It is not advised to use this particular configuration. HDR 200% increases the dynamic range of the scene's highlights by one stop. The appearance of the JPEG will be strikingly similar to that produced with DR200% and equivalent exposure parameters (aperture, shutter speed, ISO). HDR 400% increases the dynamic range of the scene's highlights by two stops. The appearance of the JPEG will be strikingly similar to that produced with DR400% and equivalent exposure parameters (aperture, shutter speed, ISO). HDR 800% increases the dynamic range of the scene's highlights by three stops. In the X-T5, no equivalent DR setting exists. HDR 800%+ functions similarly to HDR800 but augments the JPEG with supplementary shadow dynamic range and a marginal quantity of additional highlight dynamic range through the internal RAW processing of the tone curve, which is flattened. Additionally, it seems to modify the CLARITY parameter internally.

CONTINUOUS Low/ HIGH ES (BURST)

Motion can be captured in a series of images.

- To select either CL (low-speed burst) or CH (high-speed burst), rotate the drive dial.

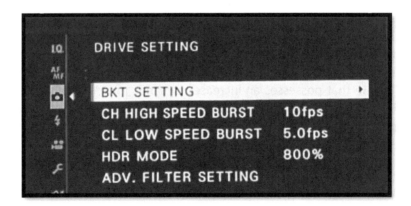

In the SHOOTING SETTINGS menu, select DRIVE SETTING and then select a frame advance rate.

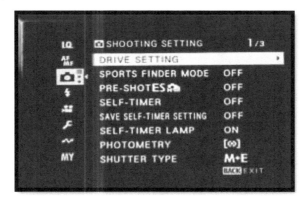

By maintaining pressure on the shutter button, the camera will sustain its photo-taking operations. When the shutter button is released or the memory card is complete, shooting ends.

Bracketing

Vary settings automatically across a series of images. Change the drive dial setting to BKT. In the SHOOTING SETTINGS menu, select DRIVE SETTING and then choose one of the following: AE BKT, ISO BKT, FILM SIMULATION BKT, WHITE BALANCE BKT, or DYNAMIC RANGE BKT.

Take photography

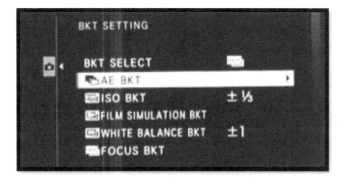

AE BKT

AE BKT SETTING is determined by shooting setting > drive setting > BKT SETTING. To determine the number of bracketing shots, turn the dial clockwise. With each press of the shutter button, the camera will capture the designated number of photos: one that is exposed according to the meter value, and the rest are overexposed or underexposed by factors that are multiples of the bracketing amount that was selected. The exposure metering system, despite the number of bracketing, will not allow exposure to go beyond its limit.

ISO BKT

A bracketing amount of ±1, ±2/3, or ±1/3 needs to be decided upon. With each shutter release, the camera will capture an image at the current sensitivity and perform a processing operation to generate two additional copies: one with the sensitivity level at the target, and the other with the sensitivity reduced to the same level.

FILM SIMULATION BKT

When you press the shutter button, the camera will generate duplicates of such photo using the film simulation settings selected via SHOOTING SETTING > DRIVE SETTING > BKT SETTING > FILM SIMULATION BKT.

DYNAMIC RANGE BKT

The camera captures three images with varying dynamic ranges for each press of the shutter button: The first shot is 100%, for the second shot 200%, for the third shot, and for the fourth shot 400%.

Panorama

To create a panorama:

- Rotate the drive dial to you
- Press the left selector to adjust the camera pan angle during shooting. Select a size and press MENU/OK.
- To display a choice of pan directions, press the selector to the right. Highlight a pan direction and press MENU/OK.
- To start recording, Press the shutter button down
- Pan the camera in a direction indicated by the arrow. The shooting process stops automatically when the camera reaches the end of the guide and the panorama is complete.

Motion panorama

Motion Panorama functions similarly to the panorama feature on a smartphone: the X-T5, for instance, can be used to shoot a series of images and finally stitch them together into a panoramic JPEG file as the camera is moved either horizontally or vertically. Pressing the panorama button on the DRIVE dial will select panorama mode and offer the two diameters (M and L) and the direction of the panning motion (left, right, up, and down) for selection. The vertical motion can be pictured differently by the use of the perpendicular camera.

The following are several suggestions for optimizing the outcomes of motion panoramas:

JPEG PANORAMA is the only output of the motion panorama; hence, the white balance and film simulation parameters of the camera have to be configured before capturing the images. The exposure, white balance, and focusing parameters, similarly, are all kept constant during the entire motion panorama recording process. These are indeed valid for all modes of focusing, including MF, AF-S, and AF-C. Therefore, establishing a depth of field and focus distance that is suitable for the entirety of the panoramic scene is important. Panoramas tend to encompass a broad expanse, characterized by diverse lighting conditions and abrupt contrast shifts. It is prudent to shoot with an extended DR setting, such as DR200% or DR400%, in such situations. Furthermore, it is important to adjust the exposure to complement the entirety of the panoramic image rather than focusing on a specific portion of it. Motion panorama is compatible with all four exposure modes; therefore, manual mode M may be the most preferred choice. Please be aware that motion panorama functionality is limited to multi-metering. Shift the camera toward a representative portion of the panoramic scene, then half-press the shutter button to secure focus, exposure, white balance, and DR if you choose not to set these parameters manually. Then, while holding the shutter button half-depressed, proceed to the desired location to initiate the panning action. At that location, fully press the shutter button to initiate the panning motion. Remember that to secure the exposure of the panorama by half-pressing the shutter, SHUTTER AE must be set to ON.

Suppress highly dynamic scenarios. Ghosting anomalies can occur when moving objects (people, vehicles, etc.) appear (partially) in more than one location of the final panorama. Adhere to a prudent distance from the panoramic scene. Avoid capturing panoramas from close range. Additionally, ensure that adequate depth of field is present. For this task, wide-angle lenses are more suitable than standard or telephoto lenses. Ensure that the shutter speed is sufficiently quick to prevent panning-induced motion distortion. Avoid pan-setting too rapidly! Pace the EVF (camera held to the eye) at all times; never use the LCD (arms extended in front of you) to do so. Stand parallel to the panoramic scene and on level ground at all times while panning. Make an effort to disregard any potential time lag that may transpire between the image presently being captured and the one that is exhibited in the eye-piece viewfinder (EVF). Maintain a steady motion while panning the camera until it ceases capturing frames. Please ensure that the camera is leveled to the horizon using a tripod. Immediately examine the completed panorama in the viewfinder of the camera once it has been captured. Be on the lookout for ghosting artifacts and embroidery errors. Perform this action while you are still on location, not when it is too late to reshoot a failed panorama at home.

Other Drive Modes (Not in Drive)

Pixel-Shift

In this mode, the X-T5 captures 20 images by adjusting the image sensor by a half-pixel with each photo using its in-body image stabilization (IBIS). Each frame is captured in RAW format. The RAWs must then be combined using the free Fujifilm Pixel Shift Combiner software to produce a DNG file with a 40 MP or 160 MP resolutions. This DNG file is ultimately compatible with Lightroom and Capture One. Additionally, this DNG file will have a greater dynamic range than a single-frame.. Choose an interval setting after selecting SHOOTING SETTING > PIXEL SHIFT MULTI SHOT to enable Pixel Shift Multi-Shot. Typically, the SHORTEST INTERVAL should be selected in this case. Upon the deactivation of the shutter button, an electronic shutter (ES) will commence operation, capturing all twenty images with identical focal distance and exposure configurations.

Multi Exposure

Multiple Exposures generates a composite JPEG or HEIF file by superimposing up to nine separate images. Additionally, individual RAW files are saved for each photo, allowing for external processing and overlaying of the shots on a computer. The function can be enabled by navigating to SHOOTING SETTINGS > MULTI EXPOSURE > ON and selecting one of the available overlay options (ADDITIVE, AVERAGE, LIGHT, DARK).

Sports Finder Mode

Sports Finder Mode crops the resulting image by 1.29x. A vibrant white frame is used to denote the crop in the live view. Sports Finder Mode is exclusively compatible with the electronic first curtain shutter (EFCS) or mechanical shutter (MS). Enabling visibility beyond the final image frame can assist in minimizing reaction time when confronted with situations involving abruptly appearing moving objects in the live view. During Sports Finder Mode, the camera's automatic focus tracking capabilities transcend the bright frame indication, enabling the monitoring of objects situated beyond the active image region.

Pre-Shot ES (Burst) - Action Bracketing

The "time machine" functionality of Pre-Shot ES enables you to capture instances that were just missed. It operates exclusively in conjunction with the high-speed burst mode (CH) and electronic shutter (ES). Using the electronic shutter and new processor of the X-T5, Pre-Shot ES enables burst mode settings with a 1.29x compression and speeds of 10, 13, or 20 frames per second. Additionally, 8.9 or 13 fps can be used without a crop. The X-T5 initiates image recording and buffering in Pre-Shot ES mode when the shutter release button is half-pressed and held. Maintaining the finger halfway down will cause the camera to continue capturing images in its buffer. It will continue to refresh the buffered content by the FIFO (first in, first out) principle, ensuring that the buffer always contains multiple frames. When an abrupt occurrence is captured by fully depressing the shutter button, the camera will not only generate quality images from that point forward but also add the previously buffered images to the memory card. While maintaining the shutter release at its deepest position, the camera will proceed to acquire and add new images to the card. Pre-Shot ES enables users to effectively retrace their steps and capture the exact moment or moments preceding the complete depressurization of the shutter release button. Ordinarily, the photographer and camera would be unable to capture those instances because of the unavoidable reaction time. SHOOTING SETTING > PRE-SHOT ES > ON will activate Pre-Shot ES, but only if the camera is configured for ES-only and CH high-speed burst shooting.

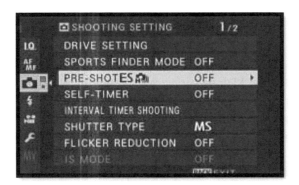

Exercise

1. Describe the different bracketing settings
2. What is pixel shift
3. Describe the sport finder mode

CHAPTER 8

EXTERIOR CONTROLS (USERS & SETTINGS)

Primary Exposure Controls

Three primary parameters affect an image's exposure: ISO, shutter speed, or aperture. The aperture, shutter speed, and ISO settings are the main exposure controls used while taking pictures. These modifications directly affect how much light enters the camera sensor, which in turn affects how bright or dark the image is. While this was touched on in passing in the previous chapter, let's go into more detail now. **For the PSAM exposure modes, including Auto ISO, which lets the camera choose the ISO, you can manually set the ISO.**

- In P, Program mode, you configure ISO, and the camera helps with the modification of shutter speed and aperture (f/stop) to create exposure. This sometimes is regarded as the Program AE.
- In A Aperture exposure mode, you configure ISO and aperture (f/stop) through the Aperture ring/switch. The camera will then control the shutter speed. This is sometimes known as Aperture Priority.
- In M Manual exposure mode, you control ISO, shutter speed, and also aperture. The camera also displays its thoughts on the accuracy of your proposed exposure just where the EV scale usually is in P, S, A, and M modes but then it relies on you the user to help modify the settings manually.

Aperture Ring

A cursory glance at the Fujifilm XF lens series reveals that certain lenses have marks carved on their aperture rings, whereas other lenses' aperture rings do not. Regardless of whether the ring's markings are etched or not, spinning the ring allows you to adjust the aperture in 1/3rd stop increments. Furthermore, some lenses feature an aperture ring that can be rotated away from the A position to activate the A Aperture Priority mode, while other lenses require the rotation of a separate switch off the A position. (To be deemed aperture priority, the shutter speed dial needs to be set to A.) If you set the aperture to anything other than A, the camera will enter the Aperture exposure mode, where you can modify the aperture in steps of one-third stop. (You must set the shutter speed to A). Press the A button on the lens aperture ring or switch and move the shutter to A to put the camera in P program exposure mode.

Shutter Speed Dial

The shutter speed dial is the name given to a physical dial or control seen on certain cameras. The shutter speed can be manually adjusted by the photographer using this dial or control, which is located on the camera. The majority of cameras with it are ones with manual exposure control or manual shooting modes. One of the main exposure controls on the XT5 is also the shutter speed dial. It is indicated in full exposure stops, and the numbers etched on it indicate how to rotate this special dial to shift it from one full stop to the next. You only need to move the rear command dial to either increment or decrement if 1/3rd stop increments are required. Keep in mind that the dial needs to be set to A for the P program AE mode. You can choose between 1/3rd stop increments and 1/8000th of a second for shutter speed increases in S Shutter aperture mode in any other location.

250x-Flash Sync Speed

All cameras have a maximum shutter speed, which varies from one camera to the next, at which they may take flash photos. For the gadget, this is known as "Flash Sync Speed." The "Flash Sync Speed" of the X-T5 is indicated on the dial that regulates the shutter speed, and it may go up to a maximum of 1/250 of a second. Of course, there is a method for taking flash photos at shutter speeds quicker than this one, and you may also take them at shutter speeds slower than this one if you'd like.

Time

Time allows shutter speeds in 1/3rd stop increments from 1/8000 of a second to 30 seconds. After that, it can accommodate shutter speeds in 1-stop increments from 30 seconds to 15 minutes. Reducing the quantity of information displayed on the shutter speed dial and making it more user-friendly for shutter speeds greater than one second are its main goals. However, when shooting in S mode, you can use this option as an electronic shutter speed change if you'd like. You have to stabilize your camera before you hit the shutter button to capture a picture with a slow shutter speed. A countdown timer starts and a big, flashing red dot appears in the display to alert the user not to touch the camera for any length of time that the exposure duration is more than one second.

Bulb

Several various cameras have a mode called "Bulb" that allows the user to manually control how long the camera's shutter is left open. The shutter remains open in the Bulb mode as long as the shutter release button is depressed. This allows for longer exposure times than are often achievable with the standard range of available shutter speeds. Make sure you are in full manual exposure mode by manually setting your aperture and selecting B on the shutter speed dial if you want to take a Bulb picture. Bulb as a word will then be displayed in the viewfinder where previous shutter speed numbers show. You need to be aware of a "special" case of BULB: the duration of the BULB is always 30 seconds when the shutter dial is set to "B" and the aperture dial to "A." In the same way, as in TIME mode, you can press the shutter button to begin the countdown. The functionality of this peculiar "B" mode indeed is the same as the "T" mode.

ISO Dial

The ISO dial found on the outside of cameras enables you to modify the ISO sensitivity setting. This feature is one of the prominent features of the XT5 although, if you do not like making use of this dial, you can choose to soft-switch ISO with another dial.

Exposure Compensation Dial

The exposure compensation dial makes it possible to rapidly and conveniently adjust the exposure settings without having to manually adjust the ISO, shutter speed, or aperture. With its help, you can easily adjust exposure or create purposefully different exposures, giving your photos the look and feel you desire. You can adjust the brightness of the picture by turning the dial. By simply moving the dial, exposure compensation is accessible in P, S, A, and M modes. After you're done, make sure you remember to get it zeroed in. Since everything on the XT5 is displayed in real time, you will notice the brightness change right away. Note that there is a "C" etched somewhere on the dial. The Exposure Comp setting will now be controlled by your front Command Dial once you have this (Custom) configuration selected. It provides a method for soft-switching between exposure compensation levels and is easy to use. Furthermore, Custom EV provides ten (minus five) stops of reimbursement.

Manual Exposure Mode

This mode is the result of three external camera controllers operating simultaneously. You have effectively assumed full control over exposure when you shift the shutter speed, ISO, and aperture from their "A" positions. You have control over the ISO, aperture, and shutter speed while using the manual mode. You also have the option to select Auto ISO, however doing so will force you to exit the manual control mode. You will then need to manually configure the settings, even though the camera will still show your current settings as the correct exposure on the exposure compensation indicator and the histogram. It is crucial to remember that all you are doing is manually adjusting the camera to accomplish what it would have done automatically if you simply adjusted the manual exposure so that the indication shows what the camera views as a "normal" exposure.

Focus Mode Selector

The focus mode selector is a control that can be found on most cameras and it gives you the ability to choose the focusing mode that you want to use for your photographs. In the XT5, It gives the user the option to switch between the autofocus (AF) modes (AF-S and AF-C) and the manual focus (MF) mode.

AF-S (Single AF)

Most cameras are configured with the autofocusing mode called "Single AF" as the default. The shutter button can be used to lock focus on a subject when it is only partially depressed. If you hold the shutter button halfway down for an extended period after the focus is locked, the distance won't change. If the sound happens to be turned on in

Menu > Setting > Sound Setting > AF Beep Vol.,

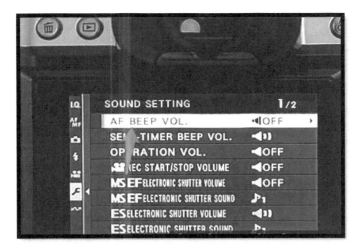

 You will be able to hear an audible chirp which will confirm that the focus is locked. The focus frame switches from white to green with focus, and is then accompanied by a much higher-visibility confirmation bright green focus indicator located on the left side of the finders.

AF-C (Continuous AF)

Continuous AF" (AF-C) is an autofocus mode that makes an effort, while the shutter button is being held down halfway, to keep whatever is behind the white focus frame in focus. To put it simply, the AF-C algorithm attempts to keep focus on a moving subject by anticipating that it will be moving. As long as you keep your subject in line with the focus frame, it works well for photographing moving subjects like animals or children. Regardless of the kind of subject you are photographing, this is true. The focus is continuously altered by the camera, therefore unlike AF-S, the focus frame will not always stay green to show that the camera has locked focus. When combined with the X-T5's increased processing power and the use of phase-detect pixels for AF-C, the algorithms have become so good that you can expect your focus to stay fixed on a stationary target even if the subject moves. Furthermore, to promptly switch to a new target whenever the camera (or focus frame) hovers briefly over the preceding one. In this setting is embedded another setting which you ought to have a perfect understanding of; release! You can access it by clicking on

Menu > AF/MF > Release / Focus Priority

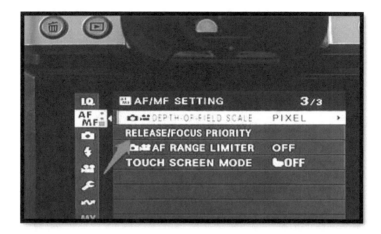

Whether or whether the camera is focused, if you fully press the shutter button, the image will be captured in AF-C mode. When "focus" is selected, the camera waits to take a picture until the AF-C system verifies that the focus has been reached. Point your camera at a stationary object where AF-C is at a disadvantage (it's expecting motion, remember) and snap a photo of it, and you might be able to see the difference in the amount of time it takes when using "Release" and "Focus". "Focus" takes a little longer, but the outcome is unquestionably of far higher caliber. It is significantly more difficult to observe when the subject is moving.

MF (Manual Focus)

Just as it sounds, it is manual and has no autofocus. The camera is embedded with some nice MF assist features to ensure shooting in this mode is very easy and accurate. Note also that you can tap the AF-On button in MF mode and the camera will then autofocus enabling the tweaking of the manual focus forthwith.

Sync Terminal (PC Sync)

The PC Sync connection standard is used in photography to synchronize cameras and external flash units. It goes by the names Sync Port and Sync Terminal as well. It makes it possible for the flash and the camera to communicate with one another so that the flash will activate precisely when the camera's shutter opens. The XT5 is equipped with a flash sync terminal, sometimes known as a PC sync port. Although many flash units include PC ports, they can use a PC sync cable to trigger flashes or studio strobes exclusively. This cable is commonly used to connect studio strobes rather than accessory flashes.

Left Doors

The connections for external microphones, headphones, USB, and HDMI are the only uses for the left door.

Two connectors are shielded by the top flap;
- The top socket is used for an external microphone.
- The second is used for remote release.

The bottom flap helps with the protection of two more;
- The top is a type C HDMI port.
- The lower socket is used for micro-USB 3.0

Microphone Jack

Microphone jacks, also known as audio jacks or headphone jacks, are used to connect microphones, headphones, and other audio devices to electronic devices such as computers, cellphones, and audio equipment. Another name for this type of connector is an audio or headphone jack. The device's connector is occasionally referred to as a headphone jack. But the guide that comes with the camera says you can't use microphones that need to be plugged in for electricity. You must utilize an externally powered microphone with a separate power supply. Note however that if you are making use of an external microphone, there is a need for you to configure the audio recording level per

Menu > Microphone > External Mic Level Adjustment.

Remote Release

This gadget allows photographers to remotely activate a camera's shutter without having to contact the sensor directly. Other names for a remote release include a remote control or remote shutter release. It allows photographers to shoot images without shaking the camera, which is particularly helpful in situations when even a small amount of movement could result in a lower-quality image.

HDMI

High-Definition Multimedia Interface, or HDMI, is a commonly used technology that enables the transfer of uncompressed digital audio and video signals in high quality across different devices.

High-definition and ultra-high-definition content can now be sent using HDMI as the standard link. The X-T5's HDMI implementation accomplishes more. In addition to shooting videos, you may also take still photos by connecting to external monitors. An external monitor connected to the HDMI connector will show what the viewfinders are seeing when still photography is being done. The studio would be the most advantageous place for this to be used.

USB-C-Headphones, Charge, Connect

Helps to provide connectivity so that images can be sent, the camera can be operated remotely or by tethering, settings can be backed up and restored, RAW files can be converted using Fujifilm X RAW Studio, and the camera's internal battery can be charged. The USB port can be used for charging the camera's battery while it is inside the device, printing photos to a compatible printer, backing up and restoring camera setups, and taking in USB-C headphone adapters for headphones. The standard procedure for attaching a USB cable to a device is to turn the device off first, attach the cable, and then turn the device back on. Allowing the camera to recognize the cable when it is initially turned on, will shield it against unintentional electrical triggers and improper connections.

DRIVE Dial

This is used in the selection of a stills shooting mode and has been extensively discussed in the previous chapter.

Delete Button (TrashCan)

This has the symbol of a trash can; it is used to delete one or many images that are no longer needed from the memory card. It can also be used to delete videos also.

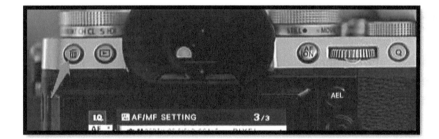

Playback Button

This button is used to play pictures and videos that have been saved in the camera.

Viewfinder

A viewfinder, which is an optical or electronic attachment for a camera, allows the photographer to arrange and organize their shots. It gives the photographer an instantaneous view of the world through the lens of the camera, enabling them to make compositional decisions regarding focus, framing, and overall composition before capturing the picture. The diopter setting of the X-T5 provides a helpful correction range (-5 to +3m-1) for mild long- and short-sightedness (hyperopia and myopia). This may help you focus the scene more clearly and enable you to use the viewfinder without wearing glasses. When you wear glasses, light can flow through the lens and into your eye. This often results in glare from reflections, making it challenging to see what you are focusing on. Furthermore, the view via the viewfinder gets increasingly constrained. To read a screen full of text, just align your eye to gaze through the viewfinder, press the MENU button, and adjust the diopter dial until the writing is as clear as possible. This will finish the diopter correction adjustment. If your vision is only slightly off, you should try both wearing and not wearing glasses to see which works best for you. Astigmatism is another prevalent eyesight issue that needs to be adjusted for using complicated optics. Diopter correction does not help in any way with this condition.

Film Plane Marker

For technical applications that need an accurate measurement of the distance between the sensor and the subject, the Film Plane Marker identifies the location of the sensor plane.   It is necessary to know the exact distance between the subject and the film plane (the sensor in a digital camera) to achieve an appropriate exposure, which is why the Film Plane Marker is employed under challenging lighting conditions. The exact distance from this marker to the subject is what is used to determine the focus distance.

View Mode & the Eye Sensor

The display setting or mode known as "View Mode" controls how the camera's back LCD screen or electronic viewfinder (EVF) functions. Another name for it is "view mode." This function allows you to adjust how the camera shows the live-view image while you are creating and reviewing your shots. The Eye Sensor is a sensor found on cameras, and it is located next to the electronic viewfinder (EVF). It's built to detect whether one of your eyes is visible when you gaze through the viewfinder. The camera will automatically turn on the electronic viewfinder (EVF) when it detects your eye and turns off the back LCD screen to provide a seamless transition between the two viewing modes. With mirrorless cameras, this feature is quite useful because you can use the LCD screen on the back of the camera or the electronic viewfinder (EVF) to compose and assess your shots. The Eye Sensor can help conserve battery life by turning off the electronic viewfinder (EVF) and the rear LCD screen when not in use. Furthermore, it responds to the presence or absence of the user's eye by alternating between the two viewing options, which enhances the natural and unobtrusive nature of the shooting experience.

Still/Movie Mode Dial

Just as the name implies, this dial chooses between shooting photos which are known as still, and movies. When the switch is done, it modifies the menu of the camera i.e. what the camera can shoot and what the shutter button can do when it is pressed.

AF-On Button

This enables you to tap or swap the button to lock autofocus. Use the AF Lock Only setting to lock the focus. In the beginning, this does not automatically focus. Use AF-On to your advantage in this regard. Despite the absence of an AF-On switch. You have to keep pressing the button in the autofocus mode if you want to stop the camera from focusing on its own when you press the shutter. The AF-On button may lock the focus in three different ways, and you can modify the function button settings to suit your preferences.

AF Lock only

In this mode, locking focus at the focal length the lens is focused at is facilitated by pushing the AF-On button. The focus will remain locked even after you take the picture if you choose to utilize the toggle approach with the AE-L and AF-On buttons. All you have to do to shoot the next picture with locked focus is press the shutter button. Naturally, if you press the AF-On button one more time, the focus will be unlocked.

AF-On

This option autofocuses and also locks focus only while the button is being held. It ignores **Menu > Settings > Button/Dial Setting > AE/AF Lock Mode** and acts as though it is pressing or there is a momentary switch. As such, if you would like to have a back-button focus flow, this is the go-to setting for you.

Instant AF

Instant Auto Focus (also known as Instant AF) is a feature that can be found in some cameras, the most common of which are mirrorless and digital single-lens reflex (DSLR) cameras. It is intended to provide a performance that is both quick and precise while utilizing the autofocus function to guarantee a quick and accurate focus acquisition when capturing still photos or filming videos. Using advanced autofocus algorithms and technologies, the Instant AF feature quickly determines the focus distance and adjusts the lens focus to match the measured value. When attempting to catch action that is happening quickly or when the subject is moving quickly, it is extremely useful. In the XT5, this feature helps so many users keep their camera in manual focus mode and then makes use of the AF-On button for back-button autofocus and with focus peaking around the corner.

AE-L Button

The Auto Exposure Lock (AE-L) button is a widely used feature present on several cameras, including the Fujifilm XT5. When you want to maintain consistent exposure for multiple pictures or while you are recomposing your shot, you can lock exposure parameters like ISO, shutter speed, and aperture. When you want to capture multiple pictures in the same lighting situation, this is helpful. A lockable exposure button in a convenient location is desirable, as not all scenes are the same and do not reflect an average brightness of 18% to the camera. Additionally, a subject is not always centered in the frame, nor is it lighted uniformly with the background surrounding it; therefore, it is necessary to select the exposure that is most suitable for the subject you are photographing. When you press the **"AEL" button**,

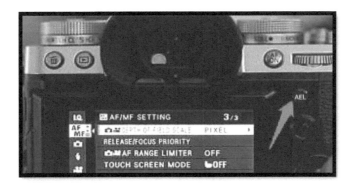

The exposure is locked. This means that the camera will remember the ISO, f/stop, and shutter speed that you choose (it works in P, A, and S modes), and these settings will not change no matter where you aim the camera. After recomposing the shot by moving the camera in different directions, you can then capture the picture.

Front & Rear Command Dials

Oftentimes, all cameras come with two command dials. One helps with controlling the shutter speed while the other controls the aperture.

The following are the roles of these dials in the XT5;
- When playing back, the front dials advances to the next or previous image, while the back dial facilitates easy zooming in or out to view thumbnails of the images.
- The two knobs of a menu navigate between the different menu choices. While the rear dial navigates through the items on the current page before moving on to the next, the front dial navigates through the menu item pages.
- Only the back dial in the Q-menu can go through the choice with highlighted features. Still, the touch screen responds very quickly.
- Focus Frame; in this option, the two dials help to alter the size of the focus frame.
- In the shooting mode, you are at liberty to determine what you would like the dials to control.

Joystick - Focus Stick/Lever

The joystick/focus stick (lever) on the X-T5 offers a greater range of capability than on any other X-T camera that came before it. When you push and hold the joystick for an extended period, a menu will appear that gives you the option to choose between pressing the stick and tilting it.

Disp/ Back/ Bluetooth/ Fn Bluetooth

The data displayed in the shooting displays will be updated when you push the DISP button. Regarding the BACK button, if you press it when at the top of the menu, it will either take you back to the previous page or exit the navigation completely. Pressing and holding the Bluetooth button will initiate the pairing process or turn Bluetooth on or off. You can quickly change the function that is typically assigned to any Fn button by long-pressing it. The DISP/BACK buttons function as a back key in some menus, returning you to the previous menu screen. Backing out of the menu returns you to the previous screen if you are already at the top of the menu.

Fn Buttons & Gestures

With just swipes or the use of a button, you can access the menu functions with ease. Long pressing the DISP button springs up a screen ensuring it is convenient to alter the button options.

Indicator Lamp

A tiny light-emitting diode (LED) or incandescent bulb used to provide visual feedback or transmit data regarding a device's state or operation is called an indicator lamp. Another name for it is a status light. An indicator lamp is sometimes known as a status light or an indicator light. The XT5's indicator helps change the color to display the camera's status. There isn't much of it because the colors and flashing vs. constant status are typically not thought to be employed consistently or in line with traditional color shading. However, keep in mind that a color does not imply that you are free to shoot. When the focus is locked, the color green has the same meaning as it does in the viewfinder. When the camera is turned on, a steady flashing red and green light appears. An orange hue flashes steadily until the buffer is filled. A memory or lens error is indicated when the camera flashes red. The indicator lamp will never come on while you are staring through the viewfinder. The indicator lamp will never come on while you are staring through the viewfinder. When charging a battery, the indicator bulb remains on; when the battery is fully charged, it shuts off; and if there is an issue with the battery, it blinks.

Other Controls

The other controls that can be found in the XT5 include; the OIS switch on certain XF lenses, the flat hot shoe, inbuilt microphones and speakers, batteries as well and memory cards all of which will be discussed in different sections of this unique book.

Exercise

1. Capture a picture with the use of the shutter speed dial.
2. With the use of the focus mode selector, choose the preferred mode you would like to shoot a picture.
3. What is a microphone jack?
4. Assign functions in the camera to the Q-button.
5. What is the function of the indicator lamp?

CHAPTER 9

STILLS LIGHTING (FLASH)

The technique of lighting a subject during still photography that makes use of artificial light sources, including strobes or dedicated flash units, is called "stills lighting," which is also known as "flash lighting." This is a common method for controlling and enhancing lighting conditions in a range of shooting scenarios. Flash is the only light at your disposal, and the quality of light is more important in photography than its amount! Hence the requirement for you to understand the use of Flash.

TTL VS Manual Flash

The ability to employ Flash automatically or manually, depending on what suits you most, is one really special feature. Additionally, you have the option to have both and then decide which one provides you with superior flash quality. You'll understand the notion of manual flash much better once you've mastered it. By choosing an output from full flash power to 1/128 flash power, you can change how much light the flash produces (the output that produces the least amount of light changes according to the flash unit).

TTL Flash

"Through-The-Lens" (often shortened to "TTL") is a word used in flash photography to describe a metering system that automatically adjusts and monitors the flash output following the exposure and metering settings on the camera. Another way to shorten TTL flash is "TTL flash." It's a technological development that allows for automated flash exposure control, which greatly simplifies the process of taking correctly exposed flash photos. Given the current ISO, f/stop, and shutter speed, your camera can calculate how much flashlight is needed to generate a suitable exposure because it only knows how much ambient light is being reflected from your subject. When it recognizes this, it can tell the flash how much light to produce to snap the necessary picture. All you need to do is configure the controls of the camera to expose the background and then make use of the flash to add light to the foreground subject.

Flash Compensation

A function of cameras and flash units called flash compensation enables manual adjustment of the flash's output power to adjust exposure. It is used to adjust the flash's intensity to get the desired lighting effect or to balance the flash against surrounding light.

Compared to previous "X" cameras, the X-T5 boasts a 2-stop integrated flash correction that can be adjusted in 1/3rd stop increments. For your convenience, you have the choice to attach this to the Q-Menu or an Fn button.

Flash exposure can be varied depending on what you are doing;
- In a dimly lit room, you can use 0 if the flash is the predominant source of light (90 percent or more of the total). This will almost certainly not produce a high-quality photograph, but it will produce an image. If you are familiar with how to drag the shutter, you can switch to manual exposure, set the flash exposure to -1 or higher, and produce some results that are worth looking at. The slow-sync flash mode can be of assistance to you in this regard as well.
- If you employ a bounce flash or a white piece of paper to mix flash and ambient light, you may want to adjust this to -1/3rd (or more) so that the outcome appears more "natural" and less like it was taken with a flash. This will help reduce the appearance of artificial lighting.
- If you are making use of the fill flash on a day that is quite sunny to lighten shadows on faces, you can choose to configure flash compensation to -1/3rd or much more.

When the flash is ready to take a picture, the finders will display a number and an icon that looks like a flash to indicate the flash compensation amount. When the flash is ready to take a picture, the finders will display a number and an icon that looks like a flash to indicate the flash compensation amount.

Manual Flash Mode

When the flash is ready to take a photo, the finders will show a number and an icon that resembles a flash to indicate the flash compensation amount. When the flash is ready to take a photo, the finders will show a number and an icon that resembles a flash to indicate the flash compensation amount. When there is an automatic option, people frequently wonder why a manual flash mod is still necessary. Whether to utilize manual flash mode or TTL (through-the-lens) flash mode depends on the particular shooting situation, the amount of control you want, and the convenience you want. Each approach has advantages and considerations of its own.

There are several reasons why the manual flash mode might be preferred over TTL, some of which are as follows:
- **Control and Consistency**: With manual flash mode, you can precisely adjust the desired flash intensity because you have direct control over the flash output power. When precise control over the flash output is required for artistic purposes or when it's necessary to maintain consistent lighting effects over multiple photos, this level of control is extremely helpful.
- **Predictability**: Since the manual flash mode does not entirely rely on the camera's metering algorithm to estimate the flash's output, it offers a fairly consistent and

predictable flash output. This can be a useful feature if you need to photograph under constant lighting conditions or if you need to maintain a specific look without having to adjust for changes in ambient light or subject reflectivity.

- **Flash-to-Subject Distance**: Manual flash mode enables you to modify the output of the flash output power depending on the flash-to-subject distance manually. This can be quite beneficial when having to work with subjects at varying distances or when making use of various flash units in diverse positions.

Getting Flash off Camera

It takes the manipulation of light to get the flash off the camera. This gives you more control over where the light comes from and how much of it is shaded than the built-in flash could ever hope to. If you do this, your photos will have an air of mystery about them right away. Many people experience anxiety while using wireless flash, although this is unfounded. Even though the procedure is not expensive or complicated, the outcomes are very convincing.

Off-Camera Key Concepts

There are a few fundamental ideas that one should be familiar with before beginning to work with off-camera flash or off-camera lighting setups.

The following are some significant ideas to keep in mind:

- **Direction of Light:** Light coming directly from the top of the camera helps to create a flash-lighting effect. Basic to all wireless flash photography is obtaining light to fall on the subject from somewhere aside from where the camera is which makes it quite interesting.
- **Ratio Lighting and Flash Groups**: Additionally, the best lighting is typically that which illuminates a topic disproportionally. This is sometimes referred to as ratio-lighting, and words like key and fill lights are used.
- Having multiple flash units that send flash power of varied intensities to the subject of the shot is the best way to accomplish ratio lighting when utilizing off-camera flash. You would just turn one flash's power dial down relative to another while utilizing a manual flash. This also holds if you use a wireless TTL flash.

To get the perfect lighting ratio for the subject, flashes are typically grouped so that the camera can simply manage the power of each group. The fill lights have a lower intensity compared to the key lights. Even fewer rim lights may be necessary, depending on the creative impetus that lies behind the composition. The ratio of key light to fill light is frequently set at 2:1. Although this is not set in stone in any way.

Off-Camera Methods

There are quite several ways to separate your camera and flash. Below are some of them;
- **C (commander legacy manual)**: this makes use of manual flash with the legacy commander infrared wireless triggering system of the camera.
- **Radio (Manual)**: this makes use of the manual flash with wireless radio triggers.
- **Cable (TTL)**: this makes use of cables and also keeps TTL flash metering.
- **Fuji TTL**: makes use of Commander (Optical) infrared wireless of Fujifilms.
- **Radio (TTL)**: this makes use of the wireless radio triggers of Fujifilm with the Fujifilm EF-60, or makes use of a this-party TTL flash system.

Commander-Legacy Manual IR Wireless

Commander is the "legacy" flash mode for Fujifilm. Infrared (wireless) flash with off-camera manual flash exposure is a feature of the early X cameras. The simplest wireless flash is this one. When properly configured, the EF-X8 or EF-X500 shoots slave flashes with a flash of light. The triggering pulse can interact with a flash by reflecting off a wall, ceiling, or subject, but the "master" and "slave" flashes must be in direct line of sight. In addition to being wire-free, IR wireless flash enables "slave" flashes to be positioned anywhere they can "see" the triggering pulse. Add as many slaves to the scene as you choose! IR wireless is less reliable outside than indoors/studio. Two reasons. The triggering signal reflects off fewer objects in bright sunshine, making the line of sight even more important. There are advantages, though. Quick IR. There is no flash unit dialogue or delay in signal propagation. It thereby fits the cable for accurate, fast shutter operation. Naturally, the most ideal but least dependable scenario for the triggering system is when ambient sunshine is balanced with flash. It functions nicely if it does. Commander (legacy) requires a minimum of two flash units. An infinite number of compatible manual slave flashes are at your disposal. These flashes can be positioned anywhere as long as they are within the master unit's signaling range to receive the signal that initiates them. It is not too vulnerable to harm.

Follow the steps below to get this working;
- Position the triggering flash unit atop the camera and then switch it on.
- Navigate to **Menu > Flash Mode > Flash Function Setting then choose Commander (legacy) mode**.
- Engage commander mode on the flash for the master flash.
- To use slave flashes, switch them to wireless mode. Make sure the flash on top of the camera is sending signals to them. Take a shot as a test.
- Next, individually modify the flash exposure for every single flash unit. The histogram can be used to do this. With an EF-X20, turn the exposure dial to one of the six settings to manually adjust the white balance. The TTL flash, which is incompatible with the mode, is controlled by the red settings in wireless Commander Mode.
- You can proceed with shooting only if you are certain that you have sufficiently followed the directions above.

- Once you are done shooting, ensure you take the flash configuration of the camera back to TTL Flash (fill flash) so it will work well as you expect the next time you get a hold of the camera.

Manual Flash- Radio Wireless Triggering

This is another unique way to separate flash and camera. Some of its main benefits include;
- No line of sight is needed (for instance, pop receivers/ flashes in softboxes, around corners, etc, and also the use of hidden flash).
- Eligible to cover more distances.
- They are in no way prone to sunlight like IR hence it is very good for outdoor shoots.
- They do not need wires ripping out or tripping over.

TTL-Fly by Wire Cables

Even if you connect your Fujifilm accessory flash to your camera via cables, your automated flash metering will still function. This keeps the ease of having light on your camera while enabling you to make use of some of the advantages of off-camera flash use. The most obvious drawback of using wires is the wires themselves. Their operating range is fairly limited, they have several physical contacts that can go wrong, and they are easy to trip over.

Fujifilm's TTL Commander (Optical) wireless system

The Commander (Optical) IR wireless trigger system from Fujifilm is an optical and infrared TTL/HSS wireless trigger system that is fairly similar to wireless trigger systems used by other manufacturers. Since using an optical system helps to alleviate cross-jurisdictional radio problems, it has long been advised. Among the causes is this. That being said, it has a wide range of applications. Working with rapid shutter speeds requires the absence of radio transmission delay, which is something that IR triggering lacks.

TTL-Radio Wireless Triggering

Using TTL (Through-The-Lens) metering, TTL-Radio wireless triggering is a wireless communication method that makes it possible to remotely activate off-camera flash units. It creates the ideal blend of automatic exposure control from TTL Flash and the ease of wireless triggering. One convenient and versatile solution for off-camera flash photography is TTL-Radio wireless triggering. It gives you more creative control over your shots by allowing you to remotely control and automate flash exposure. This adapter simplifies the task of managing several off-camera flash units and adds automatic TTL flash control for added convenience.

FP High-Speed Sync

Facial plane high-speed sync, or FP(HSS), is not to be confused with Real High-Speed Sync (RHSS), which is a feature of X100 cameras. Because of the way their leaf shutters are made, these cameras have extremely high maximum flash sync rates. The X-T5 on the other hand, features a conventional focal plane shutter with much slower maximum flash sync speeds. The fastest shutter speed at which the focal plane shutter of a camera can expose the whole imaging sensor to a single flash pulse is known as the maximum sync speed. The fastest shutter speed at which maximum sync speed may be attained is this one. Above this point, increasing the shutter speed will cause a black band to appear in the image as part of the sensor is covered up when the shutter shuts. The X-T5 has a "Flash Sync Speed" that can go up to a maximum of 1/250 of a second. Of course, if you want to, you may take flash photographs at shutter speeds that are slower than this one, and there is also a way to take flash photographs at shutter speeds that are faster than this one.

HSS benefits

The real benefit of HSS lies in its capacity to rival existing natural light sources, especially sunshine. Sunlight-produced images usually feature unappealing shadows and are harsh, flat, and poorly illuminated. HSS allows one to achieve a balance between the use of flash and natural light, even when shooting in the middle of the day in bright sunlight. This setting causes the shutter speed to pop to keep that bright ambient light in check, especially when combined with the requirement to use wide apertures for better bokeh (low depth of field, background blur).

Flash Power

Flash power is the term used to describe the amount of light produced by a flash unit. Lighting a subject correctly is crucial because it controls the amount of output or brightness that the flash will produce. To achieve the right exposure and keep total control over the lighting in your photos, you must have a working understanding of flash power. It is important to remember that several factors, including the flash unit's capabilities, the power settings, the distance between the flash and the subject, and the use of light modifiers, can impact the flash's potency. Furthermore, the flash power may have an impact on the flash duration, which may then have an impact on how well the image freezes motion. You can have a higher amount of control over the lighting in your images if you have a solid understanding of the flash power and its many control choices. You will be able to get the necessary exposure and creative effects by experimenting with various flash power settings, flash-to-subject distances, and lighting arrangements.

Shooting HSS

Using any of the identified flashes mounted on top of the camera, or with one or more of them operating in wireless mode, you can create your own "flash tree" by shooting in high-speed sync mode. This is compatible with both the Fujifilm (NAS) wireless system, which comprises the EF-W1 trigger and the EF-60 flash, and the Commander (Optical) TTL wireless mode from Fujifilm. The Godox and Nissan systems can fire in high-strength steel. A neutral density filter can be used as an additional technique to reduce light levels in bright environments. The amount of flash power required will be further decreased if you use one with an HSS flash. Why? Adjusting the flash compensation by the amount of stops the ND filter is filtering will correct the lighting of your subject without significantly changing the background lighting since you are most likely utilizing flash to light a subject in the foreground.

Flash Options

Fujifilm offers six different versions of auxiliary flashes for purchase. Together, these components, which mount to the top of the camera, enable TTL (auto) flash. There's usually a manual flash-shooting mode as well. The camera's integrated IR wireless TTL technology works with the EF-X500; yet, a wireless kit with many EF-X500s might be somewhat costly. The new EF-60 can be used wirelessly or on camera and comes with an EF-W1 wireless trigger.

- **Manual Flash**: if you are willing to shoot manual flash, virtually any flash unit capable of manual flash will work with the XT5. Also, a full kit with triggers and about three flashes for off-camera wireless manual flash isn't so expensive.
- **Third-party flash:** if there is a need for off-camera wireless TTL (auto) flash, there are various nice third-party systems that are quite good and also cost-effective.

Fujifilm Accessory Flash Models

Fujifilm offers a range of auxiliary flashes that may be purchased to work with their X-Series mirrorless cameras. These flashes are adaptable enough to be used in a multitude of photographic situations and provide an assortment of additional lighting options.

Some of the most well-known auxiliary flash models produced by Fujifilm are as follows:

- **Fujifilm EF-42**: The EF-42 is a more advanced external flash with a much higher guide number. It offers a versatile range of features which includes TTL flash control, manual power control, and also a motorized zoom head that modifies its coverage from 24mm to 105mm.
- **Fujifilm EF-X500**: This external flash was designed for professional and advanced photographers, and it is fairly powerful. With a high guide number of about 50(m/ISO100), it also offers a lot of functions, such as wireless remote control, support

for high-speed sync (HSS), TTL flash control, and weather-resistant design. The cutting-edge X-series cameras from Fujifilm are also compatible with the EF-X5OO.

- **Fujifilm EF-60**: Fujifilm only started selling the wireless EF-60 flash with the EF-W1 wireless trigger recently. If you've been watching third-party goods, you'll quickly notice that this trigger looks a lot like the one on the Nissin i60 and the Air10s.

Third-Party Manual Flash Models

The same N/P wireless (IR) protocol that the X-T5 utilizes to activate Fujifilm flashes while it is in legacy Commander Mode may also be used to initiate manual flashes. However, as no TTL metering is provided for manual flash devices, you will have to meter them manually. They do, however, trigger, and most other third-party lights that may be triggered by infrared triggering will presumably also react. Furthermore, low-cost triggering devices are available, like the Yongnuo YN560-TX II remote manual controller. With this controller, you may set up the manual flash output on your camera for up to six groups of YN flash units. If the more reasonably priced YN-660 flash better meets your demands, you may also choose it. Which integrates into a single handy device the capabilities of a YN 560 IV and a YN560-TX controller. Because of its integrated triggering mechanism, this flash may be used as both a flash and a flash controller, enabling you to operate up to six groups of compatible flash units.

Third-Party TTL Flash Models

There has been a significant increase in the number of third-party wireless TTL flash systems introduced onto the market in the past few years, which is one of the most interesting advancements. Although there are a number of them, the two brands, Godox and Nissin, are the ones that are often used.

Nissin

Nissin's radio-triggering system is called the NAS (Nissin Air System), and it can directly drive flashes that are compatible with it. Flashes from different brands, such as Canon and Nikon flashes, can be controlled using TTL receivers that are compatible with each other. Additionally, if you have many Nissin flashes, you may use an AIR 10s trigger to control the flash fleet from a variety of camera systems. This is possible if you utilize a Nissin flash fleet. The i40 and the i60a are the Nissin flashes that have provided me with the most opportunities for hands-on practice. The i40 is a compact flash that may be mounted on top of a camera to provide fill light. In addition to its compact size, the GN60 i60a features an integrated receiver and may function as an outstanding and strong off-camera flash. It is a lot more compact than other flashes with the same amount of power.

Godox

Godox sells a range of flashes that work with Fujifilm cameras, in addition to the XProF trigger, which is also compatible with Fujifilm cameras. Again, you can manage the same Godox fleet from various camera manufacturers thanks to interoperable triggers. I've had the chance to experiment with two Godox flashes: the TT350F and the V860IIF. Because the TT350F is not significantly larger than the Nissin i40, the camera does not appear absurdly small. It requires two AA batteries to operate, but it does a good job of filling flash when working up close. The V860II has a substantial power output. It is powered by a Li-ion battery that lasts a long time and recycles quickly, and it has a big form factor and strong power output.

Exercise

1. Differentiate between TTL and manual flash.
2. Shoot a picture in manual flash mode.
3. What are HSS benefits?
4. Mention 2 third-party flash models.

CHAPTER 10

LENS CONSIDERATIONS

There are several factors you should take into account when choosing lenses for your camera to ensure that you get the lens that best suits your needs as a professional photographer. Given Fujinon's long-standing reputation as a leading manufacturer of glass for use in security, broadcast (TV), movies, medical, binoculars, scopes, and other industrial applications, you have every reason to believe that the company will develop high-quality camera lenses. Furthermore, it seems like Fujifilm has already decided that XF lenses will be "good," in contrast to other manufacturers! Down to the so-called "kit lens," as they call it.

XF vs. XC vs. MXK Lenses

As you may have seen, the XF, XC, and MXK lens ranges are all compatible with Fujifilm's X cameras. The cameras that the XF Lenses are intended to be compatible with are the X-Pro, X-T, X-E, and X-H series. Pancake lenses have higher maximum apertures and are frequently faster than XC lenses. All of them have an aperture ring on the lens, except the original 27mm pancake. "What the "C" in "XC" stands for is "compact." The cameras that are most appropriate for using XC Lenses include the X-M1, X-A series, and X-T10/X-T20/X-T30 (as well as further models). Because these lenses lack aperture rings, you have to spin the camera's command dial to adjust the aperture. This helps to reduce the size of the lenses and increases their portability. As you may have seen, the XF, XC, and MXK lens ranges are all compatible with Fujifilm's X cameras. The cameras that the XF Lenses are intended to be compatible with are the X-Pro, X-T, X-E, and X-H series. Pancake lenses have higher maximum apertures and are frequently faster than XC lenses. All of them have an aperture ring on the lens, except the original 27mm pancake. "What the "C" in "XC" stands for is "compact." The cameras that are most appropriate for using XC Lenses include the X-M1, X-A series, and X-T10/X-T20/X-T30 (as well as further models). Because these lenses lack aperture rings, you have to spin the camera's command dial to adjust the aperture. This helps to reduce the size of the lenses and increases their portability.

Between these different lens classes, there is a fair amount of overlap in terms of focal lengths. In comparison to the 18-55mm zoom, the field of view provided by the XC 16-50mm F/3.5-5.6 OIS is far more expansive. However, it begins at F/3.5, making it a "slower" aperture. Compact and lighter in weight, XC lenses are frequently superior to XF lenses. One advantage of using XC lenses is this. The 16-50mm XC lens weighs approximately 195 kilos and is only 65 millimeters long. With apertures ranging from F/3.5 to F/5.6, it is "slower" than its XF counterpart and has fewer glass components (12 total). By contrast, the XF 16-55mm lens measures 106 millimeters in length, weighs 655 grams, and features an aperture that is always fixed at F/2.8. It is far more than glass, with 17 distinct components. XF lenses offer the advantage of being fast, having a high IQ, and matching the latest X cameras' shooting quality. Furthermore, lenses with Fujifilm's High

Transmittance Electron Beam Coating, like the XF 16-55mm, are included. This coating uses a technique known as "Nano-GI" (Gradient Index) coating technology, which reduces the quantity of light entering at an angle by altering the refractive index between glass and air. All of this is done to reduce flare and ghosting and enhance image quality even more.

Fast Glass

Numerous Fujifilm still lenses are fast, meaning they feature large apertures like F/1.2, F/2, and so forth. These lenses are excellent for working in low light or achieving a narrow depth of field because of their wide apertures. Increasing speed is the main result of these technical breakthroughs. Speed in autofocus, especially in the camera's ability to detect contrast quickly, and speed in processing the substantial amount of data that the 40 megapixels provide. Increasing speed is the main result of these technical breakthroughs. Speed in autofocus, especially in the camera's ability to detect contrast quickly, and speed in processing the substantial amount of data that the 40 megapixels provide. Compared to prior lenses, this more contemporary "fast glass" can focus on the X-T5 faster. The 35mm F/2 is one of these new lens types. If you have access to both the new and the older models, you can do side-by-side tests to see how the differences impact your photography. You will most noticeably see this difference in regions where phase detection isn't working effectively, or, to put it another way, when the camera depends a lot on contrast for autofocus. This behavior is also noticeable while shooting high-speed burst shots tracking fast action, which is a scenario that puts a lot of strain on focusing. All-weather sealed "fast glass" lenses are getting more and more popular; they are made to work with the newest "X" cameras.

Fixed-Focal Length Prime Lenses

The conventional defense of employing prime lenses with fixed focal lengths is image quality. Consistency in quality is unattainable for zoom lenses across their entire zoom range. The softest images are typically produced by zoom lenses at their maximum aperture and zoom settings. To obtain the best possible image quality, many people choose to pack a wide range of prime lenses in their lens bags. Fortunately, Fujifilm is aware of this problem and has created a wide range of fast and bright prime lenses that preserve superb image quality even at wide apertures. Longer focal length lenses are usually required for portraiture; examples of such lenses are the Fujinon 50mm F/1 or any of the 56mm F/1.2 variants. You can take some artistic shots with this lens since its F/1.2 aperture allows for a narrow depth of field that is similar to that of an F/1.8 lens on a full-frame sensor.

Zoom Lenses

There is a vast selection of zoom lenses available, and they may be used for anything from wedding photography to sports photography to bird watching. Optical image stabilization (OIS) is a very useful function to have when handling a 1.6 kg lens by hand, but not all lenses offer this feature. One somewhat new model is the XF150-600. An excellent weapon for those races in which classic cars are competing. Not only is this camera great for taking pictures of wildlife and sports, but it also has fast autofocus and clear photographs.

Power Zoom Lenses

Recently, Fujifilm unveiled the XF 18-120 F4 R LM PZ WR Power Zoom Lens, a new lens with the slogan "Make moving memories." It is stated that this lens is meant to be used only by filmmakers, or "for content creators and image-makers with a penchant for motion..." As a result, this lens was "designed in collaboration with FUJINON cine and broadcast lens designers," not an MKX. With the click-less aperture ring on this lens, you may operate the aperture smoothly and silently while filming. This capability is exclusive to this lens and is usually only used for video work. It also features controls on the lens for zooming in and out. There are several features that lens enthusiasts will adore in addition to the zoom. 7 rounded iris blades for smooth, circular bokeh; weather resistance; fluorine coating for protection; 3 ED elements to banish fringing and chromatic aberrations for clarity and color; 3 aspherical elements to combat distortion; and all of this in under half a KG, with constant F/4 at a very handy 27-183mm FF range.

MKX Cinema Lenses

With its HDMI port, inbuilt 4K/DCI/6.2K recording, and unique video menus and modes, the X-T5 may be the go-to camera for anyone working on big video projects. This suggests that there would be value in discussing serious video lenses. Professional videographers are thrilled to hear about Fujifilm's MKX lenses, which further validates the company's commitment to creating high-end platforms for still photography and video. T2.9 is the constant aperture of the two cine lenses (18-55 and 50-135). Should you be a stills-focused photographer, you may find yourself confused by the latest hype. If you work as a cameraman, you are aware of how important this issue is. Taking static photos is very different from taking videos. Even little changes in exposure, angle of view, and axis orientation are visible when watching a video. Consequently, the goal of the design of these cine lenses is to minimize the amount of focus and optical axis shift that happens during the zooming process, as well as the amount of noticeable angle of view change that happens in lenses when subjects are drawn into focus. Furthermore, each lens is what's known as an all-manual cinema lens, which means that, unlike a still lens, it doesn't use autofocus but rather requires the user to manually pull focus. Lastly, rather than F-Stops, cine lens apertures are measured in T-Stops. T-stops consider both the aperture and the lens transmittance to more accurately determine exposure. The T-Number printed on one lens can be used in place of the T-Number printed on another lens, to put it briefly. You know that in regards to the aperture numbers, this is NOT the case. The viewer may easily notice even the smallest change in exposure in videography because images, or movie frames, are shown in rapid succession. This seemingly small differential has important implications.

OIS -Optical Image Stabilization

Several of Fujifilm's zoom lenses have optical image stabilization built in, which the firm claims can provide an advantage of up to five stops. Lenses use onboard processors and gyro sensors to achieve this, allowing them to detect even the smallest frequency of camera wobbling. The lens makes its adjustments by moving its constituent parts 16,000 times per second. Fuji talks about their "Drift Tracking" OIS technology, which only takes signal "shakes" out of the signal. As was previously said, OIS is especially beneficial when used with long zoom lenses because this is the type of lens that makes the camera shake the most evident. However, it is also handy with wide-angle lenses, as it has the added benefit of being able to take useful photos at very low shutter speeds.

AF Range Limiter

The Range Limiter limits the focal range that the lens will search for focus over when auto-focus is activated. When the subject's distance is known, this is useful. Think about taking pictures of stars, portraits, sporting events, macro photography, and so on. The autofocus range limiter on a camera only limits the range of distances the camera will try to focus at. The camera will not even try to focus outside of this range. This search inside a constrained radius improves one's speed as well as their capacity for concentration and attention. Macro lenses, which focus anywhere can from a few centimeters to infinity, typically come equipped with range limiters. When the limiter is engaged, the lens will disregard the macro focal length and instead only search for focus across a "normal" focus range. There are also range limiters available for some telephoto lenses. This will focus the lens on the objects in the distance while ignoring the subjects in the foreground. You may have observed that occasionally your camera will hunt across the entire focus range when it is unable to lock focus. The environments with either very little light or very little contrast are where this happens most commonly. The time required to accomplish this task would be significantly decreased if the camera "knew" to only chase focus within a predetermined range of distances. You can now use this feature with any lens that can autofocus because an AF Range Limiter has been included in the camera body. Additionally, this usually entails dealing with topics that lend themselves to telephoto or macro photography.

Teleconverters

Teleconverters complete the line of Fujifilm lenses. They offer a lens focal length multiplier of either 1.4 or 2X and are weather-resistant, which puts them in line with the more recent lenses. It would be oversimplifying the problem to say that adding a teleconverter to the light path has no impact on the image quality. Every time a piece of glass is positioned in the flow of light, it affects the level of intelligence. Nevertheless, the cost—whatever it may be—might be more than reasonable given the longer focal length and the possible quality of a lens with such a long focal length.

Third-Party Photography Lenses

Since the release of the first Fujifilm cameras, an increasing number of third-party lenses designed specifically for manual focus have become available for use with these cameras. There has also been a massive increase in the quantity of autofocus lenses available in recent years. For Fujifilm photographers, this is very exciting news because it offers a variety of lenses with the option to focus manually or automatically. This implies that you can obtain the lens of your choice.

M-Mount

Fujifilm has admitted that owners of M-mount glass may desire to use their costly investments on their X cameras. This is a possibility that the company has acknowledged. To that end, make an M-mount adapter available as an optional extra. Electrical contact is established between the lens and the camera utilizing the adapter, which also automatically triggers the "Shoot without Lens" mode on the camera.

Adapting Legacy Glass

Heritage glass, which refers to older lenses with aperture rings, is easier to adapt than most current glass. No, things aren't much easier. The steps are nearly the same, but now you have to cope with an accurate aperture ring labeled with f/stops. This will enable you to precisely adjust the lens's aperture. This implies that legacy glass that has been adapted can be used with your X-T5. Since you are using modified lenses, you are officially using stopped-down (Aperture) mode when taking pictures. Nevertheless, the camera will automatically switch to Aperture priority mode since it detects that you are manually adjusting the aperture. You don't need to worry about adjusting the ISO or shutter speed unless you wish to because the exposure is good enough.

Lens Modulation Optimizer

The Lens Modulation Optimizer (LMO) technology is a feature of Fujifilm's X-Series mirrorless cameras, which the firm developed in-house. Its design will also lessen the effects of lens aberrations and diffraction, improving the overall sharpness and quality of the image. After light passes through the lens and comes into contact with the sensor, it is possible for diffraction and lens aberrations, such as distortion, chromatic aberration, and spherical aberration, to affect the light that is caught by the camera. These conditions may cause the image's sharpness and clarity to decrease. The Lens Modulation Optimizer mitigates these effects, leading to an overall enhancement in image quality. The Lens Modulation Optimizer was created specifically to be used with lenses made by Fujifilm. The camera system can recognize the installed lens and will utilize an optimization profile tailored to that particular lens. This ensures that the adjustment will be customized to the unique optical characteristics and possible issues of every lens. Fujifilm employs both RAW processing software and camera hardware that includes a Lens Modulation Optimizer. The optimization will be applied automatically throughout the capturing process, and further fine-tuning can be carried out during post-processing using the RAW conversion tools from Fujifilm, including the company's proprietary RAW file converter. It is significant to remember that the Lens Modulation Optimizer function is exclusive to Fujifilm's X-Series cameras and lenses. It might not be available on other camera systems or lenses made by different manufacturers. The Lens Modulation Optimizer was developed to assist photographers in attaining the highest possible image quality by correcting difficulties that are caused by lenses. Enabling this feature on Fujifilm X-Series cameras and lenses can help increase overall image quality as well as sharpness and detail, particularly when shooting at narrower apertures. This is especially true when the feature is combined with the X-Trans CMOS III image sensor.

Exercise

1. Differentiate between Power zoom lenses and zoom lenses.
2. What are teleconverters?
3. What is a fast glass?
4. What is an AF range limiter?

CHAPTER 11

MOVIE GUIDE

With the X-T2, X-H1, T3, and 4, then stepping things up with the X-H2s and ultimately arriving at the X-T5, Fujifilm has put a lot of time and effort into getting videographers interested in its products. With the ability to capture still images in 4K/6.2K HLG/F-Log (2), these cameras become valuable tools for filmmakers, showcasing many of Fujifilm's advantages in still photography. The inclusion of specialized menus and a Stills/Movie dial shows how seriously Fujifilm is taking the development of hybrid cameras. Furthermore, this is not just an aesthetic issue. Some pretty incredible advances in technology make movie mode possible. Specifically, 4K/6.2K can be externally or internally stored on memory cards; 10-bit internal recording with F-Log/F-Log2 feature A ton of movie-specific menus and settings that are only available when the camera is in movie mode, a dedicated Movie Q menu, soft-touch movie control, cine lenses with linear focusing, power zoom lenses, dedicated cine film sims, and robust color science with access to all film simulations for in-camera color grading without the need for extensive post-production Zebra, slow shutter speed settings, MPEG-4, H.264, and H.265 encoding, time coding, tally lights, and AF-C tracking are some of the extra features available in video mode.

The Quick Guide

Follow the steps below to shoot movies on the XT5;
- Select **Movie on the Stills/Movie dial** to shoot the video.
- Ensure **both the shutter speed as well as the apertures are kept on A for automatic exposure**. If you would like to have more control, you can select Aperture Priority mode by dragging the Aperture ring/switch to a configuration asides A.
- You can choose to manually **configure exposure** although this is not very straightforward like shooting stills, it's still quite easy.
- Set the microphone level record level in **Menu > Audio Setting**

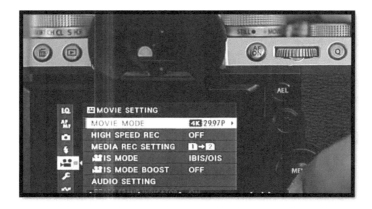

Internal/External Mic Level Adjustment

- You have three options for focusing: manually, using AF-S autofocus before you start shooting, or using AF-C for autofocusing similar to that of a camcorder.
- When filming a movie, you can freely move the focus frame. Anywhere in the composition, a much better AF-C is guaranteed with full PDAF coverage.
- Before and during the movie shoot, use the touch screen to drag the focus frame.
- The memory card can hold Full HD, 4K/6.2K, and F-Log/F-Log2/HLG movies. Instead, try a Film Sim.
- You can boost EVF /LCD brightness for outdoor shooting.

Following the methods outlined above, you will be able to utilize the XT5 to shoot whatever movie you choose.

Playing Movies on the LCD

The DOWN arrow on the rear control pad of the camera is used to start the playback of movies.

The following items allow you to control the playback of a movie:
- By pressing **DOWN**, you can resume playback from the previous pause and pause the current movie. The movie can be progressively advanced or rewinded by using the left and right arrow keys while the video is paused.
- You can fast-forward and fast-reverse the video while it's playing by pressing **LEFT and RIGHT,** respectively. A quick succession of presses will result in much faster playback, albeit with some choppy playback.
- The sound is turned off by pressing **UP.** This is not a pause in the proceedings. Restarting the movie will start it from the beginning just like the first time.
- The **OK/MENU** button allows you to adjust the playback volume level. Press the **same button to advance** to the next level after using the arrow keys or one of the dials to get there. This can be done while the playback is already paused or while it is still playing, in which case the audio will stop.

To 4K/6.2K or Not

The X-T5 can record video in both 4K and 6.2K resolutions. The section below will throw more light on what 4K is!

What is 4K (ETC)

Let's start by discussing the term "4K," which is also sometimes referred to as Ultra HD, UHD, or 2160p. The concept of "4K" originates from the resolution being approximately 4000 pixels wide.

The term "4K video" is commonly used to describe footage that was shot at a resolution of 2160 by 3840 pixels. This nomenclature states that the number 1080 represents Full HD, the number 480 represents HD, and the number 4160p represents 6.2K, which has a resolution of 6240 by 4160 pixels. Meanwhile, the number 480 represents 480 by 720 pixels. The push for 4K (or higher) video resolution stems from problems that occur when watching 1080p HD digitally captured movies on a theater screen. Customers who are watching close to the screen will see a softer, or even slightly pixelated, image due to the 1080-pixel height as opposed to the sharper projections from analog (film) movies. For this reason, there is a push to have video resolutions of 4K or higher. Although very few real clips shot on personal cameras ever make it to theater screens, this led to the establishment of a new standard (actually, several, but that's another story) and made 4K something to aim for. The field of videography has undergone a revolution thanks to the readily available high-quality still cameras that can also record video. Therefore, 4K had to be included in these cameras sooner rather than later, or else manufacturers would run the risk of lagging behind the rivals, who, as you are well aware, are constantly trying to outdo you.

F-Log, F-Log 2 & HLG

Using F-Log (Fujifilm Log) or F-Log2 when shooting video is similar to shooting stills in RAW format. The best degree of tone and dynamic range is preserved when recording using a logarithmic curve because the digital data is distributed according to the logarithmic function's setting. It preserves information in the shadows that you can use to process the image and create a wider tone range with more depth and color. This is similar to taking HDR stills. You will be recording with a linear picture profile if you don't use the log feature. Furthermore, it can be difficult to evaluate your film while you are shooting it or while you are playing it back if your display does not support LUTs. This means that you have to have a very high degree of confidence in the exposure that you have selected, regardless of whether you are shooting in F-Log or F-Log2. If you record a video in the F-Log format, after you've finished recording, you'll need to grade or post-process the footage on a computer using the relevant editing software. A LUT, also called a Lookup Table, is needed to decode the data that was collected. Should you fail to apply the appropriate LUT, your video will look flat and boring. Fujifilm's website offers an appropriate LUT for you to download.

Film Simulations for Video

The X-T5 offers very good in-camera color grading if you don't want to spend a lot of time post-processing in F-Log or HLG; just select a Film Sim and let the camera handle the rest. You'll find that this is an excellent substitute for F-Log, and it yields great results. Video color science is another area where the X-T5 seems to shine, much like still-subject imaging. The X-T5 recognizes this by coming with the dedicated "Eterna" cinema film sim, but you are still able to use any other sim you choose. You can also change the settings of the sim you choose for videography differently from those for still photography. This makes it simple to switch between taking still images and videos, using different Sims for each kind of content.

Other Neat Things the XT5 Brings to Video

- **Touch vs. Dials**: To use a touchscreen to control video capture in an essentially different way, enable Movie Optimized Control under **Menu > Movie Optimized Control.**
- **Headphones**: get to listen to what you are recording. There is a need for you to make use of the USB-C audio adapter to get the best out of this.
- **Timecodes**: can be produced while filming a video to enhance synchronization in scenarios involving multiple cameras; this should be very helpful when it comes to editing the footage for the final product. **Menu > Movie > Configuring the time code.**
- **Slow motion:** Using Full High-Definition High-Speed Recording, slow-motion films can be produced. Additionally, you can record at up to 240 frames per second, which, when played back, is eight times faster than the standard speed.

Focusing in Movies

To Focus on movies; click on Menu > AF/MF > Movie AF Mode.

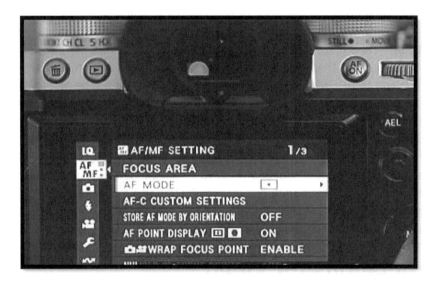

There are two focus modes for filming with the use of the XT5;
- **Multi**: this means the camera chooses the focus point it will make use of. Focus is restricted here to whatever is closest to the camera in the center of the frame.
- **Area**: this means you make a choice and the camera will then autofocus with the use of the chosen focus area.

AF-C in Multi AF mode

Multi is not the same as Wide when it comes to still photography. Instead, to keep the focus on the image when using Multi, the subject needs to stay behind the main focus area. "The camera selects the focus area automatically," according to the instruction manual, but it doesn't go into detail about how this is accomplished. My informal testing has led me to believe that the multi-zone is limited to the center of the image and that it is not very expansive, especially since there is no focus indicator. By putting a grid based on the Rule of Thirds on the screen, you can confirm this. Once you do this, you will quickly notice that a subject needs to be inside the central rectangle of the grid structure for Multi to keep it in focus. This will remain the best advice I can give you if there is no visual clue as to what Multi is looking for in its subjects.

AF-C in Area AF mode

The only difference between Area and Multi is that with Area, you have more freedom to move the focus frame around the composition. If you are careful with the camera, you can use the touch screen to rack, also known as pull focus, while you are filming by rapidly shifting the focus frame!

Touch Screen Focus

As previously mentioned, the X-T5's touch screen can be used with the Area AF mode and either the AF-S or AF-C autofocus modes. It is very similar to taking still photos in that you can use the touch screen to change the focus.

Manual Focus (Hollywood Style)

Movies can be focused manually, though there are clear disadvantages to this technique. But then, that's just how things work in Hollywood. However, "they" use a method known as focus pulling (for cross-fading), and to obtain it correctly, they meticulously measure the distance between the subject and the sensor. t should go without saying that manually focusing an LCD screen with your eyes could be challenging. But with Focus Peaking, you have much easier times. Concerning shooting motion pictures with an X camera, Focus Peaking represents a major advancement and serves the same purpose as it does for still image capture. Before proceeding, confirm that the focus selector is in the "M" position. Excessive caution is required whenever you manually turn the focus ring on a camera, as it is nearly impossible to do so without introducing some degree of wobble. The best option in this case would be to mount the camera in a configuration that includes extra hardware to move the manual focus ring. This facilitates precise, quick, and smooth focus changes by making focus-pull and marking positions very easy. This scenario and the manual focus requirements of filmmaking are precisely why the new series of MKX cine lenses was developed. In actuality, MKX cine lenses were created with this particular situation and the manual focus demands of the film industry in mind.

Controlling Movie Exposure

There are some better ways to control the amount of light that appears on screen than others. In the motion picture industry, shutter speed is crucial. It sets the amount of "frozen" or "blurred" content in each frame. This variable is directly correlated with how fluid or chaotic the footage appears. The exposure can be changed in movie mode in a few different ways, which are detailed in the following sections.

Automatic Exposure for Movies

Using automatic exposure is the easiest method to follow. All you have to do to begin recording is press the shutter button and position the ISO, shutter speed, and aperture rings at the "A" positions on their respective dials (this is equivalent to program exposure on the camera). Although you do not have direct control over the depth of field (aperture) or shutter speed when shooting in this mode, you do have the ability to manually set the ISO, much like you do when shooting stills in "P" mode. Upon switching to this mode, the exposure compensation dial will quickly become your best friend. Just make the standard adjustments to the settings for stills. Consult the histogram to determine exposure. Anytime during the filming process, you can adjust the exposure value; however, the likelihood of shaking the camera is reduced if you use Movie Optimized Control. When shooting videos with the camera set to P mode, you will notice that the aperture is constantly adjusting itself to maintain the correct exposure.

Aperture Exposure for Movies

You have control over the depth of field in movie mode thanks to the aperture exposure setting, which can also be paired with exposure compensation and ISO as was mentioned previously. **The operation of these settings is very similar to how they operate when shooting still images.**

- To use this, set **the shutter speed dial to "A"** and adjust **the aperture ring to the f/stop that you prefer**. Remember that using large apertures, like f/2, results in a significant amount of bokeh (background blurring) and shallow depth of field. Using a smaller aperture, like f/8, will result in more objects in sharp focus and a deeper depth of field. Additionally, note that your camera's specified aperture may turn to ochre-red characters when shooting in low light.

This suggests that the chosen aperture will not allow the camera to obtain a "proper" exposure. It is presumably now attempting to maintain the same exposure by varying the shutter speed and the auto ISO sensitivity (for further details, refer to the next recommendation).

Shutter Exposure for Movies

You can use Shutter AE to decrease the shutter speed or, conversely, to increase it for a more frantic "action" shot. The aforementioned effects can be achieved by combining the shutter speed with the ISO and exposure compensation settings. Using this combination is a lot like taking still photos in terms of functionality.

To use Shutter AE,

- **Set the aperture ring, switch, or dial to the "A" position, and then adjust the shutter speed dial to the appropriate value.**

Take note that the stated shutter speed can turn an ochre-red color, which indicates that the camera is unable to achieve "proper" exposure with the shutter speed that has been selected. However, in many modes, nothing will happen if you try to lower the shutter speed below the current frame rate. For example, if the shutter speed is set to 60 frames per second, it will not drop below 1/60 of a second. Similarly, SS will not drop below 1/30 of a second at 30 frames per second. This is more apparent in the overall video output quality than it is in the EXIF data. Certainly, this is the case when using the Shutter priority set.

Manual Exposure for Movies

Learning how to use manual exposure for filming movies is not difficult. As necessary, change the shutter speed, ISO, and aperture. You can make more adjustments to these while shooting to get a more accurate outcome. Unless you are employing one of the settings that have been specifically mentioned, the camera will not allow the shutter speed to drop below the video frame rate. The shutter speed can be changed in steps of one-third of a stop using the touch in Movie Optimized Control, the Q-menu, and the rear dial.

Zebra Stripes

This is a simple way of understanding the exposure that is currently being used, even though it is not an exposure mode. While the ISO and shutter speed are fixed during the shooting process, the aperture frequently controls the exposure. The majority of commercial news footage is manually shot. Finding out if something is overexposed or not can be done quickly and easily with zebra striping. When there is excessive light shining on it, the zebra pattern manifests itself.

The aperture can be made smaller to remedy this.

- Configure Zebra direction and level in **Menu > Movie > Zebra Setting and then Menu > Movie > Zebra Level.**

Thoughts on Lighting and Exposure

Since the shutter speed in video is fixed at much slower speeds than in still photography, lighting issues are slightly different in video than still photography. Considering that the ISO or aperture can control the exposure of a video, and because you should have these two settings adjusted to your preference, and because the subject of a video is usually moving, having ENOUGH light is essential. As a result, additional continuous illumination is generally utilized in the video. These days, LED light panels are not only rather inexpensive but also quite widespread and portable. In addition, the video must have the capability of capturing a moving subject while maintaining fixed lighting. Therefore, paying particular attention to the lighting is necessary while exposed to a fluid "take" under conditions that could potentially change.

Other Movie Options

In terms of movies, there are a few other options worth considering;

Metering for Movies

You have the option of using Multi, Center-Weighted, Spot, or Average metering when filming a movie. Photographing still images and capturing moving images both use a very similar metering technique.

Movie Framerate

Modifying the movie frame rate is done in **MENU > Movie Mode**.

The frame rate of movies frequently ranges from 24 to 60 frames per second. However, if you're not making a movie, any of those frame rates will work, movies rendered at 60 frames per second are sharper and clearer than those rendered at 24, 25, or 30 frames per second.

Lenses and Movie-Making

Of course, Fujifilm offers a wide variety of XF lenses, all of which are capable of producing high-quality photographs. The OIS 18-55mm lens is a very capable lens with a good range from wide to near for close-up framing. There are still more. The 56mm F/1.2 lens is perfect for portrait photography because of its small field of view and shallow depth of field. These qualities, along with its 56-millimeter focal length, could make for some interesting movie scenes. There are a few more important lens considerations to make when filming movies: The aperture is the source of the first kind of noise. The camera automatically adjusts the aperture when in P or S mode to maintain a constant exposure throughout the picture. The "ticking" sound that the camera's internal microphone records as a result of this noise is deliberate. The sound produced by autofocusing is the second problem. You can hear the lens trying to maintain focus, even though this only happens when using AF-C or when racking focus using the touch screen. The aperture must be adjusted to a fixed f/stop to separate focusing sounds. By doing this, the aperture won't produce any noise. The combination of OIS and IBIS results in the third source of noise generated by the lens. Although the exact amount of noise this factor contributes is currently completely unknown, you still have the option to disable the stabilization. Of course, additional noise elements that must be minimized include the operator's "sounds" and camera manipulation.

WB- White Balance in Movies

When working with movies, you need to adjust the white balance. All WB presets are accessible. Even better, before you begin shooting, adjust the white balance to a custom setting.

This can be done in **Menu > IQ > White Balance (Movie).**

Recording Audio & Microphones

When filming movies, the audio recording feature can be turned on or off. Also, to prevent clipping, the recording volume should be changed. There are enough built-in stereo microphones on the camera for home video production. Nevertheless, background noise, operator noise, and lens noise are all picked up by these built-in microphones and recorded in the audio. The "ticking" sound is primarily caused by the aperture; in particular, because of the frequent adjustments it makes to maintain exposure. If you take your videography seriously, you won't be able to get the quality you need from the camera's internal microphone for commentary or filming. In addition to eliminating camera sounds and background noise, adding another microphone will give the sound more directionality and depth. You might be interested in the directional stereo microphone (MIC-ST1), which is attached to the hot shoe and made by Fujifilm. It has built-in vibration reduction built into the mount to further shield the microphone from sounds originating from the tripod or camera. You are, however, in no way limited to the MIC-ST1. Numerous excellent cell phones are available that are made especially for shooting videos and can be connected straight to the camera. Some of these, like the Rode VideoMic Pro, were created specifically to be used with DSLRs and other video cameras; their functionality is designed to work best with these kinds of cameras.

Mic Adjustment & Other Audio Options

Overexposure can be used to "clip" photos, and it can also be used to "clip" audio, producing the horrible sound known as distortion.

To avoid clipping, make sure the recorded sound stays out of the "red" area on the meter. To accomplish this, go to

- **MENU > Internal / External Mic Level Adjustment. Pick either "Auto" or "Manual" from the menu.** Adjustments can be made manually between +6 and -30 dB. "Off" will turn the microphone off.

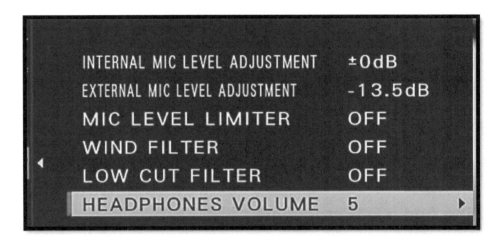

Stop Motion Movies (Stop Motion Photography)

One feature of the Fujifilm X-T5 is its ability to capture stop-motion videos (photography). It is therefore an extra way to record video. However, a large number of still photos will be taken, each requiring it's processing to achieve the desired outcome. This is a serious disadvantage. The X-H2s certainly has enough processing power to create a moving movie, but it is not capable of combining still images into one. This feature, an intervalometer, is commonly used in stop-motion photography. Their job is to time and gather a series of images that are then converted into video so that a stop-motion film can be made. This feature fires the shutter a predefined number of times, taking individual 40MP pictures and setting a predetermined interval between each shot. After that, the images can be combined. These days, stop-motion animation can be seen almost anywhere: swirling clouds dancing across night skies, chaotic cityscapes, traffic flowing like crimson rivers of blood, blood splattering like rivers, etc. It's an opportunity to try something new and let your creativity run wild with the circumstances. Not only is it fun to do, but you might enjoy taking this kind of night sky recording (assuming, naturally, that you live or visit somewhere other than the areas experiencing an increase in light pollution). In a similar vein, you can use this to record stop-motion movies with your camera of almost anything that moves—albeit slowly. Many options are available, such as crowds, water, clouds, cityscapes, and city streets.

Exercise

1. Commence playing movies on your LCD.
2. How do you know when to choose between 4K and 6.2K?
3. Make a film simulation for a video.
4. Control movie exposure with the use of the camera.
5. Briefly explain how lighting and exposure affect the outcome of your shots.
6. What is the function of white balance in movies?
7. Adjust your mic while shooting a movie to ensure that the sound is well captured.

CHAPTER 12

WI-FI, BLUETOOTH, WIRELESS & INSTAX

The X-T5 has built-in Bluetooth and 802.11b/g/n wireless networking. It is new to have 5GHz 802.11 a/n/ac wirelesses included, and there are many ways to take advantage of all of its features. Adding Bluetooth to the wireless stack allows the device to maintain a connection to a phone or tablet that has been connected to it. Through this connection, the device can receive both "background" transfers of marked images and continuous photo transfers. This is on top of the functions that are already present on bodies without Bluetooth technology, like the capacity to browse and transfer photos over a Wi-Fi network. The issue with Wi-Fi and Bluetooth is that it is possible to establish two sets of connections to a device at the same time to transfer photos and control the camera remotely. The fact that the camera will still use Wi-Fi rather than Bluetooth to upload photos may be confusing even with Bluetooth turned on. Bluetooth's main function is to keep a connection with a device so that data can be transferred seemingly seamlessly. If you would prefer not to use the transfer option for any reason, just navigate to **Menu > Network/USB > Bluetooth/Smartphone Setting > Auto Image Transfer Order > Off.**

Wi-Fi Remote Control

This special feature allows you to take pictures or record videos with your camera using a phone or tablet. This is a relatively new feature that is frequently seen in recently created cameras. The device must have a remote-control app installed on it and be paired via Bluetooth to utilize this feature.

Upon assuming that your phone and camera are paired for remote control, proceed as instructed below to begin;
- Enable **GPS & Bluetooth on the phone**. And also enable Bluetooth in the camera.
- Locate the **Camera Remote app on your phone and tap to commence**.
- Tap the **Live View shooting button on the screen of the app**. You see "Connecting" being displayed on the phone and Waiting for Connected" on the camera.
- Once a connection has been established, you can start shooting.

Note however that this feature works in portrait mode alone. If you tilt the camera to landscape mode, the app will not change its orientation.

Transfer Images from Phone

You can transfer images from the phone and also browse pictures from the phone.

To either browse or download/import images to your device, follow the steps below;

- When the app screen appears, tap **Import Image**. Various thumbnail images will fill your phone's screen once the connection has been locked. You can select the photos you want to import onto your device or click on an image to view it in a larger format.

Once the above has been completed, you can then;
- View the gallery of images on your device, or
- Touch **the small circle in the upper left corner** of a thumbnail to check it for import. You can bring in more than just one image.
- Tap **the Import option** on the phone when you are through, and images are sent to the phone.
- Tap **OK** in the top right corner of the screen to leave the phone view of the images.

Transfer Images to Smartphone

With this feature, images shot can be transferred to a device or you can also choose to create an order of images and send them.

- **Menu > Network / USB > Bluetooth/ Smartphone Setting > Auto Image Transfer Order > On**.

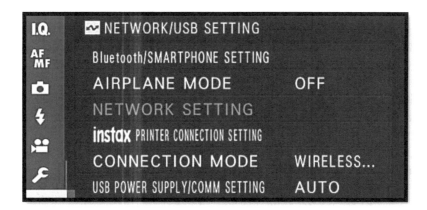

- **Playback > Transfer Image to Smartphone**.

Once the above steps have been completed you must then do the following;
- Set up the required app on your mobile device.
- The camera and the device you want to send the photos to are paired via Bluetooth.
- Turn on or off Bluetooth for the camera and gadget.
- Decide exactly how you want the photos to be sent.
- Launch the application on your phone.

If you would like to have all images transferred, click on **Menu > Network /USB > Bluetooth /Smartphone Setting > Auto Image Transfer Order > on**. With this, you can send images you shoot to your preferred device.

If you would like to use the playback option,
- To move photos, just navigate to the **Playback menu, choose Transfer Image to Smartphone, and then select the photos you want to move**. Not only can you select the memory card you want to use at this point, but you can also filter the photos that are transferred.
- After the option has been chosen, press the **BACK button**, then select **Start Transfer.** The selected photographs will be saved to the mobile device.

You should be aware that, unlike voice, which can be transferred using your car's hands-free technology, photos cannot be sent via Bluetooth. The purpose of the Bluetooth connection is only to keep the phone and camera connected. The camera and phone then seamlessly transition to Wi-Fi to finish the image transfer once the command to send is received (through Bluetooth). You will see an extremely long and unpleasant warning message when you turn off your device with Bluetooth turned off but images in a Transfer Order or Auto Image Transfer turned on. Just to be sure, turn on Bluetooth before trying to upload the Transfer Order. That's all.

Bluetooth Pairing

The pairing process is straightforward, albeit time-consuming due to the multiple displays involved. Both the phone and the camera need to have Bluetooth enabled, and the app needs to be running on the phone. (Note that the following is only compatible with Android)

To start with;
- Enable Bluetooth on the camera by clicking on **Menu > Network /USB > Bluetooth/Smartphone Setting > Bluetooth > On**.
- Move to the phone. Enable Bluetooth and also enable location services.
- Then you can open the Fujifilm Camera Remote app.
  - On the first launch, this will launch the first screen. Tap **X System**.
  - Choose Interchangeable lens camera".
  - Select **XT5.**
  - Go to **Add.**
  - Click **Menu > Network/USB > Bluetooth/Smartphone Setting > Pairing Registration** to start pairing from the camera's point of view.
  - Choose **Proceed** on the phone app. After that, this will locate the camera. Once you tap the camera's name on your phone, pairing will happen.
  - It will switch to a new screen for the camera. To accept the pairing, click OK.
  - Following that, pairing is finished.

To make use of the connection;

- Choose what you would like the connection to do on your phone. Live View Shooting provides you with a remote shooting option from your phone.

Instax Printing

This option helps with the printing of images wirelessly to Fujifilm Instax SP-1, SP-2, OR SP-3 printers. You must first go to **MENU > Settings > Print > Connection Setting > Instax Printer Connection Setting** before you can start printing to an Instax printer. After that, you must "pair" or "connect" a particular printer to the camera by inputting its password and SSID (secured ID). To accomplish this, choose "Connection Setting > Instax Printer Connection Setting." A "film" cartridge containing at least one unused print must be inserted into the printer after it has been turned on. If you have already connected your Instax camera to your Instax printer, selecting **Instax Printer Print** from the second page of the **Playback menu** will immediately begin an effort to connect the camera and printer, presuming that you have taken care of the criteria. When the X-T5 finds the printer, you want to use, the image you selected to print will show up on the screen. It will be sent to the printer when you press **OK,** and it will spit out the film after whirring for a short while. To make multiple copies of the image, you will only need to send it to the printer once. The printer prints a second (or third, fourth, etc.) copy when the copy/reprint button is pressed.

Pairing with an Instax Printer

This feature helps to establish the connection or pairing between the camera and the printer. This can be accessed by touching **Menu > Settings > Connection Setting > Instax Printer Connection Setting**.

You can also follow the setting above to pair and then;
- Select the **Instax Printer Connection Configuration.**
- Fill in the available slots with the SSID number that is printed on the bottom of your Instax printer. Make sure to include all leading zeros in the total. When finished, tap **OK.**
- Place the password in last. Just tap OK as the default is 1111. Using the **Instax Printer Smartphone App,** you have the option to modify the password.

Other Bluetooth Functions

With Bluetooth you can;

- Synchronize date and time and/or location information with the use of your phone.

- o **Menu > Settings > Connection Setting > Bluetooth Settings > Smartphone Sync Setting** then choose the option to sync your phone.
- Pair about 7 devices.
  - o **Menu > Setting > Network /USB Setting > Bluetooth Settings > Choose Pairing Destination**.
- Update the camera firmware from your device.

Exercise

1. What is the function of the WIFI remote control?
2. Control your camera with the use of the WIFI remote control.
3. Transfer images you must have captured to your phone.
4. Pair your camera and smartphone with the use of Bluetooth.
5. Connect your camera to an Instax printer and commence printing.

CHAPTER 13

THE PLAYBACK MENU

This chapter covers the range of options and functions available to you when you tap the **Menu button in Playback.** You can also access the Setup and Network/USB menus from this location.

Switch Shot for Playback

The playback immediately changes to the "other" card that was inserted. It does not affect the card that is utilized for the image capture in any way. In the unlikely event that the camera has two memory cards, which memory card do you want the replay to come from? This makes a simple switch from the card that is currently active to the "other" card. This notification lets you know which card is in use right now by saying that it's been "SWITCHED TO SLOT x." You will receive a warning saying ".!. 2 NO IMAGE" if you save every image in the sequence and one of your cards has no images on it. And speaking of messages, if there isn't a card in the other slot, a message like this one, which says ".!. 2 NO CARD," will show up. Oddly, it doesn't reverse, and even after the camera is turned back on, playback will keep trying to use the missing card.

RAW Conversion Edit Pictures In-Camera

This feature helps with the posting of a RAW file into a new JPEG/HEIF image. You can post-process RAW images (including RAWs made from RAW+JPEG or HEIF images) in-camera with this menu option, saving each newly processed image as a separate file and preserving the RAW data intact. Using the same RAW file, you can repeat this process multiple times, saving a new JPEG each time. Similar to how there are numerous settings to experiment with in "RAW File Converter" or other software programs, there are numerous settings to experiment with in in-camera processing. Select a setting to use or modify (the camera stores the settings from the original image and uses them as a basis for every adjustment you make).

- By using the **Q button**, you can view a preview of your edited image at any time. Once you have completed viewing a photo, you have two options: click **OK** to save the picture as a new file to the memory card, or click **BACK** to end the preview and begin the process.

Conversion Setting	What it Does
Reflect Shooting Condition	Uses the camera settings that were in place when the user took the picture to produce a JPEG/HEIF or TIFF file. If you had taken the photo in RAW along with JPEG or HEIF format, you would have received the same output.
File Type	Output a JPEG, an HEIF, or an 8 or 16-bit TIFF.
Image size	Modify the size of the image or alter its aspect ratio.
Image Quality	Give out the resultant image as FINE or Normal Quality.
Push/Pull Processing	Modify the exposure. This has the same effect as using the Exposure Compensation Dial to change the exposure while shooting. Equivalent to a third-stop increase. As opposed to the three stops on the EV Dial, the Push/Pull provides a range of -2EV to +3EV. This data reveals what Fujifilm believes about the dynamic range in RAW photos, and it's interesting to know!
Dynamic Range	Highlights should highlight specific details. This option will be grayed out if the original RAW image was taken at 100% dynamic range. The 400% DR option in the submenu won't be available for selection if the picture was taken at the 200% dynamic range. The options available to you here will depend on the DR level that the camera selected for the shot if you used Auto DR while shooting.
D Range Priority	Preserve the intricacy in both the highlights and the shadows. If the DR prerequisites outlined above are not met, additionally unavailable.
Film Simulation	Even if you shot in RAW+ with a film simulation already applied, you should still apply a film simulation to the final image.

White Balance	Make sure the white balance is adjusted to one of the WB presets to get your whites to appear whiter. Despite having the option to select "Custom" WB, you must first build a Custom WB to move forward with the RAW Conversion. I'm not sure if anything similar would be beneficial.
Lens Modulation Optimizer	Adjust the image's lens according to the lens that was used to take the picture. Well-known lenses lead to improvements in both diffraction and edge focus. It is by default set to "On" during the shooting process, but this has no bearing on the RAW files.
Digital Tele Converter	You should use the crop-in effect if the photo was taken using the Digital Tele Converter. An additional choice that preserves photos in RAW format but converts them to JPEG or HEIF!

HEIF to JPEG/TIFF Conversion

It helps with the conversion of images captured in HEIF format. Choose Images you would like to convert from HEIF to JPEG or TIFF.

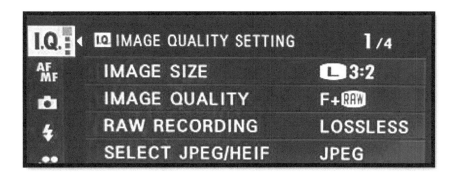

Note that format file options include; JPEG and either 8-bit or 16-bit TIFF. Make use of JPEG for uploading and TIFF for more editing. Choose a memory card you would like to save your images.

Erase

This function facilitates the erasure of a single or multiple images. Should you decide later on not to confirm the deletion by clicking **OK**, you can always undo any erasure technique that is currently in progress by lightly pressing the **shutter button.**

Simultaneous Delete

This feature allows you to delete or select not to delete JPEG/HEIF and RAW images simultaneously. When you erase the RAW image from card 1, do you want the JPEG or HEIF file on card 2 to be erased as well? Whether you were able to save the RAW photos on the first card and the JPEG or HEIF photos on the second card will determine this. ON will remove both. Choosing **OFF** does not remove the JPEG or HEIF image.

Crop

Cropping is the process of selectively removing or clipping a portion of an image to change the composition or frame the subject differently. It involves cropping out unnecessary portions of the image to change the image's size and aspect ratio.

Cropping is very simple with the XT5. You just need to rotate the rear dial to achieve the desired crop. To adjust the touch's position, steer the crop box using the joystick. Once you've reached your desired outcome, press **OK.** After the crop is stored, the new crop is shown in a playback. It is important to note that while a RAW conversion will result in a JPEG that you can crop, a RAW image cannot be cropped.

Resize

It is just as simple for the camera to enlarge or reduce the size of an image as it is to crop it. You have a choice between only three different sizes. M, S, and 640.

- Simply **select the one that you want** and then press **OK**. After that, a new image that has been scaled and given the next available image number is saved into the memory card.

If you try to resize an image that has already been reduced to a size that is less than or equal to the chosen resize, you will receive a warning. An image that is only in RAW format cannot be resized or cropped. You might think that you can, but when you try it, an error notice shows up. Still, you can adjust the size of the JPEG that was produced from the RAW+JPG. Naturally, a RAW conversion will result in a JPEG if that's what you need. The input size of the original image is the only factor that will determine the final size of the resized image. This operates in a manner that is analogous to how the cropping function does.

Protect

Errors frequently occur when you or another person is in charge of your camera. Protect your photos from being inadvertently erased while in the camera to prevent the loss of memorable images, such as those from your wedding, your best adventure, or your graduation.

- Choose **Frame, Set All, or Reset All.**

But keep in mind that photos can only be adequately safeguarded within the camera. Any other device that plugs into the memory card will expose them to the risk of deletion once more.

Image Rotate

It is simple to change the orientation of an unprotected photo before playing it back.
- Simply **pressing the up arrow will turn the dial 90 degrees to the left (anti-clockwise), while pressing the down arrow will turn the dial 90 degrees to the right (clockwise)**.
- When you are finished, press th**e OK button**.

Using the left and right arrow keys on your keyboard, you can rotate and navigate to the next and previous picture. Now that they have been rotated, images will appear in the viewfinders in the chosen orientation. Be aware that rotating an image requires you to make adjustments to it, so protected images cannot be rotated.

Voice Memo Setting

Pictures are generally useful for preserving your most treasured memories so you can revisit them whenever you look through them. However, pictures that have the voices of the people in them captured can be incredibly lovely, which is why this feature is necessary. With the aid of this feature, you can both play and add voice notes to a still image. ON facilitates the annotation of previously taken photos. Until you delete the notes, it will stay enabled and allow you to play the notes whenever you choose.
- You can see the **Recording Voice Memo on the display while a picture is playing back by simply long-pressing (for three seconds) and then holding down the front command dial.** And then you ought to speak, I see! After finishing, relax. This speech will rock the world, and you have only thirty seconds to deliver it!

Images that contain voice memos are indicated in playback by a microphone icon, and an indication that indicates you may play the image by pushing the front command dial is also displayed. Carry through those steps to view a progress bar and amaze yourself with your oratory skills. Memos are stored on the memory card in the.WAV file format, with the same file name as the image file. They require about 1 MB of storage for every 5 seconds of voice message, and they are recorded in stereo at a frequency of 48 kHz. That is almost exactly half the size of a JPEG file—nearly 6 MB for a mere 30-second recording. Though they can be added to panoramas and multiple exposures, memos cannot be added to protected images or movies. Memoranda cannot be appended to movies or images that are protected. You can remove an image's note along with it.

Rating (Favorites)

You have the option to rate the photos you have taken, which is comparable to rating online purchases. The scale for rating is 0 to 5. It is necessary to have someone rate the photos you take to avoid bias and to ensure that your assessment is accurate.

- To rate your pictures simply **rotate the rear dial to choose your preferred rating** for a particular image then touch **OK**.

Copy

An image can be practically copied from one storage location to another. Files can be copied between memory cards using this feature. After selecting Copy, you will be prompted to select which slot you want to copy from. You can then choose to copy all frames or just a single frame on a separate screen.

- **Frame**: this option prompts you with a copy icon and the question copy, ok? Positioned in the upper right of the screen. Tap the **OK** option to copy the frame/movie. The camera will automatically move to the next saved image/movie and it can also invite you to copy that image also.
- **All Frames**: this works well also and you will also be prompted as described above.

The word Storing will appear when you press OK, indicating that the camera is doing just that. The camera switches to playback mode after the procedure is complete and the message "Copy End" flashes briefly on the screen.

Transfer Image to Smartphone

This feature helps with the transfer of images to your smartphone. This has been well explained in the previous chapter.

Wireless Communication

Through a direct connection, you can connect your camera to a tablet or smartphone. Make a connection with a tablet or smartphone so you can take and view photos on the device. It can also be used with a remote control by connecting to it.

Slide Show

This option shows images that have been saved to a memory card in a specific order for a few seconds at a time; the images are only visible on the camera's LCD or electronic viewfinder, of course. Movies can also be used to play slideshows. They proceed from one to the next in an unbroken cycle.

- When the video slideshow is finished, you can exit it by pressing the **MENU button**. It is an interesting and entertaining approach to view many movie snippets that have been combined into a single film.

Photobook Assist

The ability to create books from pictures is aided by this feature. Approximately six photo books can be designed, with each book holding roughly 300 images. If you feel that you no longer need the book, you have the option to alter it by adding images (but not removing them or rearranging them) or by erasing the entire thing.

To look at a PhotoBook,

- Choose a book from the **PhotoBook menu and click "View."** To view the **"Cover" with the black frame, press the OK button**. The next set of pictures has white frames. The left and right arrow keys on the keyboard, the joystick, and both command dials can be used to move around the book. This area does not have touch control! An animation will play as you flip through the book and select different pages.

You can make a connection to an external HDTV and see your photo book in that manner. Even though the view is far more restricted than what one would get from a slideshow. To make changes to or remove a PhotoBook, select it and click the **OK button**. You can select between the Edit and Erase menus by pressing **OK once more**. In actuality, the word "editing" is a little misleading. Only the "Cover" image may be altered, and you cannot add any images or text until the very end of the book. The PhotoBook's contents will be gone if it is erased.

Print Order (DPOF)

To print photos with DPOF printers that work with your operating system, you can create a print list (order) here. Since printing photos from a memory card in a photo lab is the same process, this should also apply in theory. A standard called the Digital Print Order Format (DPOF) was created to make printing straight from a camera, without the need for a computer, easier. Note that the concept of "order" refers to the act of placing an order (just like a purchase order), and has nothing to do with the order in which photographs are added. The idea is for you to pick pictures while the memory card is still in the camera, annotate it with the DPOF marker, and then either print your choice (order) using a USB cable, insert the memory card into an appropriate printer, or bring it to the processing facility for one hour. It seems straightforward enough. And there are only two "options" to choose from: "With Date" to print the date onto each picture, or "Without Date."

Printing the Date on the Image

Printing the date on photos could be required for many reasons, including legal ones. That said, this is not a common occurrence, and it is even less common with the types of photos you will probably take with this camera. If you choose "With Date," the DPOF text that appears on the screen will be preceded by an image of a printer. Each of the photos you have selected to have printed will bear the current date once you have finished this step.

Removing DPOF & Resting All

It is possible to "unmark" an image that has already been marked to remove it from the print order.

- The print (sheets) counter in the lower left corner of the screen needs to be brought to "0" using the down arrow key after you navigate to the image, open the Print Order menu, and choose Without Date (the only option that lets you go to the next page). If you use the arrow keys to navigate to other photographs, you can remove the checkmark from those as well. Once you're done, click **OK** to see the updated total number of pages that still need to be printed.

After you have printed your images, you need to make sure that the DPOF marking is removed.

- Choose **Playback, then MENU, then Print Order (DPOF), and finally, Choose**. Reset everything, then, when prompted, select **OK** to continue.

147

However, you should be aware that the location, font size, and style of the printed date are not controlled by the camera in any way. Because the XT5 has an integrated RAW conversion engine, you can also choose to mark RAW files for printing.

Instax Printer Print

With this feature, you can wirelessly print images to a Fujifilm Instax printer. Note that this option will be grayed out if a printer has not been paired yet.

Display Aspect Ratio (DISP. Aspect)

On HD devices with a 16:9 aspect ratio, like televisions connected by HDMI cables, this parameter regulates how images with a 3:2 aspect ratio are displayed. With a 3:2 aspect ratio, the entire image is shown with black bars on either side. The image's top and bottom have been cropped to fit the screen's 16:9 aspect ratios. You cannot select this option until an HDMI cable is connected to the camera. It is grayed out. As such, you will be choosing this menu item on your field monitor or television screen.

Exercise

1. Convert a RAW file into a JPEG or HEIF image.
2. Erase a picture you are no longer in need of.
3. Delete images simultaneously.
4. Crop and modify the size of an image.
5. Include a voice memo in any of the pictures you have captured.
6. View your images using a slide show.
7. What is a Photobook Assist?

CHAPTER 14

MOVIE MENU

The Movie Menu(s) provides access to various options, which are covered in this chapter. There has been some condensing of the Movie MENU. If you select the Movie tab from the menu when using the Stills photo shooting mode, you will only be able to adjust six different parameters.

- Simply selecting **Movie on the Stills/Movie mode dial** will change the orientation of the entire menu to that of a movie.

Movie Setting

There are so many options under this menu and you will learn about each of them in the following section.

Movie Setting List

The movie settings can be accessed quickly with this menu. To modify any of the settings from this point on, simply select the desired setting and press the **OK button.** Additionally, you can select all movie recording options here, including codec, frequency 9 bitrate/MBPS; film simulation, F-Log, HLG, and RAW (for HDMI); movie media (card, HDMI); movie mode (4K, DCI), framerate (50P, etc.).

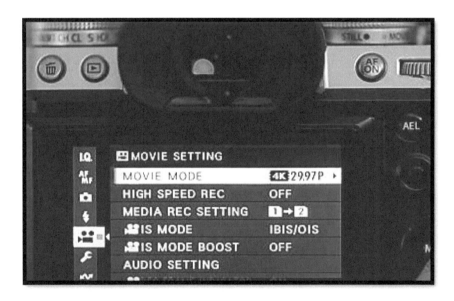

Movie Mode

You can select whether to film in 4K (HQ), 6.2K, FHD, or DCI (HQ) frame sizes with this option. Here, you can also set the frame rate and aspect ratio. However, take note that the video outputs a very large file size. Just 8 minutes of 4K (400Mbps) and 20 minutes of full HD (200Mbps) video can be recorded on a 32 GB card. These figures presuppose an H.264 codec. For the best quality and maximum compression, use 2.65.

High-Speed Rec.

Using this option makes it easier to record slow-motion footage in Full HD. Even though this feature name is technically correct, it does not effectively convey the function's intended use. With it, you can record Full HD movies in slow motion. When that movie is viewed again, the action will move more slowly. This can be used to highlight the details in a fast-moving scene or to create a purely artistic effect. Besides the OFF setting, there are four recording speeds (multipliers). One hundred, sixty, two hundred, and four hundred pence. There are limits on both the bit rate and the frame rate when it comes to high-speed recording. To make use of this option, touch **Menu >Movie Setting > High-Speed Rec**

Self-timer (for Movies)

You can choose to specifically configure a timer for your movies while you are shooting.

- **Menu > Movie Setting >Self-Timer**

Media Rec. Setting

This option will teach you how to set up how video is recorded in various types of media. This covers bitrates, codecs, compression, and how to use dual storage cards or HDMI. To make use of this option simply tap **Menu > Movie Setting >Media Rec. Setting**

There are four options to consider under the media rec setting which are;

- **Destination:** helps to configure how to make use of memory cards
- **HDMI:** helps to record to just HDMI devices alone.
- **File Type & Compression:** there are lots of settings combined here which include choosing a file format and also the choice of compression.

A video second is made up of several frames, which are still pictures. Since it is compressed, not all of the information from every frame is kept. Compressing is not a terrible concept. Practically every video you watch has indeed been compressed in some way. Blu-ray releases, social media, and television news are commonplace. There might be an impact depending on how this is done. The pilot of the X-H2(s) has two options available to them. Blockbuster filming in 4K resolution is possible with ALL-Intra. Each frame is resized while remaining in a format that allows for additional processing. It is very useful for pixel-by-pixel editing, frame-by-frame editing, and editing subjects with complex motions. It is not surprising that this puts a lot of stress on the processing hardware and the camera. An additional option for producing high-quality, 4K videos is long GOP. Because it uses a higher compression ratio, the files are eventually smaller. If complex subjects are being covered, you may or may not notice more detail. This is due to the GOP's capacity for prediction, which enables it to make informed assumptions about what ought to change and what ought to stay the same in between "I" frames.

- **Container:** the XT5 makes use of a .mov or an .MP4 container .FYI, .avi, .mpg, .mp4, .mkv, etc.

The compression method used in MOV videos was created by Apple Computer and can hold virtually any type of multimedia data, including text, audio, video, and subtitles. Using this algorithm, .MOV video serves as a sort of "container" for QuickTime multimedia files. The .MP4 format and the .MOV format are nearly interchangeable since the former formed the basis for the latter's creation. The .MP4 format is more commonly used and has been standardized globally. The QuickTime format is especially useful for editing because it doesn't require data copying. This is in contrast to other multimedia file formats, such as .MFS, MKV, and. OGG, all of which necessitate data copying. Another word that's frequently used when talking about multimedia files is container; examples are files with the .MOV and .MP4 extensions. Container formats vary amongst OSes, just as formatting a hard drive in Linux, Windows, or Mac varies slightly. In our case, ProRes or H.264/H.265 data would fit nicely within these containers because it's similar to their actual video data content being placed inside them after formatting is finished. The (.MOV) container, which is based on our example a hard drive, represents a specific movie hard drive or USB stick; the H.264/H.265 data represents its actual contents, which contain video but no audio.

Fix Movie Crop Magnification

In this option, you will be able to configure a 1.25 crop on all video footage to offer constant framing between various video modes. Once again, the name does not represent the purpose of this function accurately. Make sure that all of your video footage has the same frame by using this tool. The 4K, Slow-Mo, and Full-High-Definition videos shot with the X-T5 have been framed differently. This might not be a noticeable difference right away. Put simply, if you only use one focus and mode while filming, the results might seem cropped compared to what you get with other settings. By forcing all modes to standardize using 1.25x framing, you can avoid having to make adjustments in post-production when combining all of your footage. This should help standardize all of the frames more evenly than it otherwise would.

F-Log (2)/HLG Recording

You can designate the location of the recording's storage with this option. F-Log (2) or HLG recording is only possible when an HDMI recorder is connected. Both the locations of each and the copies of Film Sim are selectable. To gain access to this option, click on **Menu > Movie Setting >F-Log (2) / HLG Recording**

Data Level Setting

This is where you set up the signal range for recording movies. For 8-bit movies, the signal range is restricted to 16-235, and for 10-bit movies, it is 64-940. For 8-bit and 10-bit movies, the corresponding signal ranges are 0-255 and 0-1023.

- **Menu > Movie Setting >Data Level Setting**.

IS Mode

This option helps to stabilize images for movies.

- **Menu >Movie Setting > IS Mode**.

There are three options here;
- **IBIS/ OIS**: enables stabilization. Just how it is deployed is based on the specific lens and also if it is OIS or not.
- **IBIS/OIS +DIS**: Like the previous description, but with DIS (Digital Image Stabilization) added. Still images cannot be used with DIS; only moving images can. By moving the captured region farther across the sensor, DIS crops the image to enable the camera to further compensate for significant movement. Note that the footage may appear jerky at first until the sensor stabilizes itself and that the camera may interpret your attempt at panning as unintentional camera movement.
- **OFF**: here there is no form of stabilization at all.

IS Mode Boost Movies

This option helps to increase stabilization for both static and non-panning shots.

- **Menu > Movie Setting >IS Mode Boost**.

The camera's ability to stabilize images may only be slightly improved when using IS Mode Boost for movies. It is explicitly stated by Fujifilm that panning photos with this is NOT intended to be done.

Zebra Setting & Zebra Level

- Turn on the **Zebra stripe alert for overexposure**, then select **which direction the stripes should go. Adjust the minimum required level of brightness for the "Zebra Level" setting**.

While the ISO and shutter speed are fixed during the shooting process, the aperture frequently controls the exposure. The majority of commercial news footage is manually shot. Additionally, zebra striping is a simple and quick way to confirm that nothing has been overexposed. When there is excessive light shining on it, the zebra pattern manifests itself. The aperture can be made smaller to remedy this. Furthermore, you are aware of the location of the overexposure. Something that is hidden from view by a histogram. Zebra can be used in videos and doesn't require manual exposure adjustments. You can arrange the left or right zebra to help where the composition calls for it to make it stand out more. And tweak the brightness threshold further to control the appearance of striping. The zebra strips' sensitivity will drop as the setting is raised.

- **Menu > Movie Setting >Zebra Setting and Menu > Movie Setting >Zebra Level.**

Movie Optimized Control

Instead of utilizing the dials on the camera, you can choose to control various features of the movie recording using the touch screen. The turning of dials during video recording might result in noise as well as a camera shake. You can reduce the impact of these potentially detrimental effects by adjusting using the touchscreen. When you select this, you unlock an additional mode that can be used to control the camera while it is recording video, even though the only options here are On and Off. The following settings can be controlled with touch: wind filter, headphone volume, shutter speed, aperture, exposure compensation, ISO, mic level adjustments, film simulation (Movie), and white balance (Movie).

- **Menu > Movie Setting >Movie Optimized Control.**

Rec Frame Indicator

In this option, when turned on helps to show the borders of the display turn red while recording a movie.

- **Menu > Movie Setting >Rec Frame Indicator.**

Tally Light

This option helps with the control of the two tally lights of the camera. To help the camera operator and the "talent" in front of the camera know which camera is the "live" camera—also referred to as the primary camera that is recording the show—tally lights are used in television production studios. When blending multi-camera setups to produce a video for broadcast, this is extremely important. Though it may seem unnecessary at first, the "tally" light on an X-T5 has a practical purpose in informing both the subject of the video and the camera operator that the recording has started. To achieve this, this LED—which was originally intended to be used with its AF Illuminator function—now serves as both a front tally light and a rear indicator light, roles that are typically assigned to it. There are numerous options available for configuring the tally light, ranging from having both On and Off to just having one of them on.

- **Menu > Movie Setting >Tally Light**.

Select Custom Setting (presets)

This is where you select a previously saved custom camera setup for filming. Any one of the seven camera settings that have been stored in the camera's memory can be retrieved using this feature. To access this option; Tap **Menu > Movie Setting >Select Custom Setting.**

Edit/Save Custom Setting

This option helps with the configuring of custom settings for the shooting of movies. This can also be quite useful for still photography.

- **Menu > Movie Setting >Edit/Save Custom Setting**.

Wireless Communication

Helps to make use of Wi-Fi in the connection of the camera to a smartphone. Assuming the Wi-Fi Function button is mapped to this action, this completes the same task as pushing it. Connecting is another option available to you in the Playback menu. Once connected, you can take advantage of all the features offered by the connected app, such as watching videos and taking pictures.

- **Menu > Movie Setting >Wireless Communication.**

Movie Image Quality Setting

This menu has various options you will be learning about in the section below. This will help you have a perfect understanding of the various settings you are to make use of when shooting movies.

Film Simulation (Movie)

Instead of shooting video in F-Log (2) and then color grading the footage after it has been shot, take advantage of the incredible color grading that the camera already has and choose a Film Simulation when shooting movies. A whole motion picture could be shot in one of these "films". Notably, the X-T5 has the newly developed Nostalgic Neg. sim in addition to Eterna and Eterna Bleach Bypass to achieve a specific "cinema" look.

- **Menu > IQ > Fim Simulation (Movie)**

Monochromatic Color (Movie)

With this option, you can apply a warm or cool tint to black and white movies.

- **Menu > IQ > Monochromatic Color**

This option is the best and one you ought to consider if you like black and white movies.

White Balance (Movie)

You can correct for illumination that is not "pure white" by using the white Balance feature. Modify the WB, especially for the movie's filming. In addition to using one of the camera's presets you can also set or use one of three custom WB settings. Notably, WB Shift allows you to adjust WB further, and the outcome of these changes can be saved as a **Custom Setting** that can be used for the duration of filming a movie.
- **Menu > IQ > White Balance (Movie)**

Dynamic Range (Movie)

This feature helps to shoot detail in darkness while also ensuring the preservation of the highlights.
- **Menu > IQ > Dynamic Range (Movie).**

Tone Curve (Movie)

The Tone curve configuration offers much finer control over the highlights and shadows in movies. This option helps to apply a rudimentary tone curve to a movie.

- **Menu > IQ > Tone Curve (Movie).**

Color (Movie)

This option helps with increasing or decreasing color saturation.

- **Menu > IQ > Color (Movie).**

The selection of color modifies the colors' hue and saturation levels. Use this to highlight a colorful setting or to create a more "flattering" atmosphere. The "+" and "-" settings can be used to increase and decrease saturation, respectively.

Sharpness (Movie)

Watching a dull movie can be very boring. This option helps to sharpen or soften video footage.

- **Menu > IQ > Sharpness (Movie).**

High ISO NR (Noise Reduction)

You'll experience more noise problems the higher the ISO you use. It's a compromise that comes with filming in the modern era. Noise reduction can help with some of these symptoms when used properly. With its NR technology, Fujifilm argues that it can help reduce "noise in movies shot at high sensitivities (ISO)." Although "high" sensitivity is not defined, my testing indicates that ISO 800 should be regarded as the step between normal and high sensitivity.

- **Menu > IQ > High ISO NR (Movie)**

Interframe NR (Noise Reduction)

This option helps to enable noise reduction for video. It brings about the reduction of high ISO noise by about 2 stops through the comparison of noise data between frames.

Peripheral Light Correction (Movie)

This option helps to do vignetting corrections for movies for adapted lenses.

- **Menu > IQ > Peripheral Light Correction (Movie)**

It will be very helpful in many cases to realize that Peripheral Light Correction refers to vignetting adjustments. Additionally, some lenses have vignetting, which is the dark shading that shows up in the four corners of the frame. The Lens Modulation Optimization (LMO) function can automatically correct vignetting issues with recognized Fujifilm lenses by leveraging the camera's internal database. The ability to adjust for adapted lenses—lenses that the camera is unaware of—is what distinguishes this setting from others.

Mount Adaptor Setting

This feature makes it easier to adjust the settings for lenses that are connected to the camera via an adapter but are not made by Fujifilm. Modifies the surroundings for still and motion picture photography. This is also where you select the lens that will be used in the picture if it hasn't been entered previously. Instructing the camera to use that lens data to make vignetting adjustments notifies the camera of the focal length at which you are shooting (both for IBIS and to be recorded in the EXIF data).

Movie AF/MF Setting

In this menu you will learn all you need to know about focus as it has to do with movies.

Focus Area

You can specify where the focus frame will be for filming by using this option. It may seem a bit repetitive to say this. You can use the touch screen for a smaller impact or just tap the joystick to adjust the focus frame while in movie mode.

- **Menu > AF/MF > Focus Area.**

AF Mode

In this option, you can choose how the camera will autofocus when shooting movies.

- **Menu > AF/MF > AF Mode.**

There are two options here;
- **Multi**: this means the camera selects the autofocus point it will make use of which means your camera will behave just like a camcorder.
- **Area**: this means you choose. The camera focuses with the use of the chosen focus area.

AF-C Custom Setting

In this option, you get to track movies with the use of AF-C focus.

- **Menu > AF/MF > AF-C Custom Setting**.

Finally, though in a limited capacity, the AF-C Custom Settings feature—which enables focus tracking—is included in movies. Unlike the still mode, this one doesn't use any presets. Nothing more than the chance to change two tracking parameters to better fit your tastes.

For the movies option, there are two settings;
- **Tracking Sensitivity**: The tracking's "tenacity" setting is now enabled. This section allows you to control how long the camera will focus on one subject before moving to another that enters the frame either in front of or behind the subject it was previously focused on.
- **AF Speed**: this helps to determine how fast you would like the subject to come into focus when the camera switches focus to another subject.

AF-Illuminator

In this option, the camera makes use of its AF- assist LED when having to focus in dark ambient or low-contrast conditions. Setting modifies both stills and movies.

- **Menu > AF/MF > AF Illuminator**.

Face/Eye Detection Setting (Movie)

This option helps with the prioritizing of autofocus of various faces while shooting movies.

- **Menu > AF/MF > Face/Eye Detection Setting**.

MF Assist

In this option, you will get to make use of the MF assist and it includes the new Focus Meter.

- **Menu > AF/MF > MF Assist**.

Focus Check (Movie)

This setting aids in indicating whether or not the focus frame in the viewfinder needs to be automatically zoomed in when the focus ring is switched. It only functions in the Manual focus mode. Focus Zoom has a feature known as "Focus Check." Make sure the focus ring is in the "On" position if you want the viewfinder to fill with an enlarged image of the focus frame every time you turn it. "Off" maintains a vision that is not magnified.

Instant AF Setting

Here, you can select whether you want to focus manually with AF-S or AF-C. In Manual Focus Mode, the AF-C button facilitates instantaneous autofocus.

- **Menu > AF/MF > Instant AF Setting.**

Depth of Field Scale

In this option, you can select a depth of field display methodology for shooting. Note however that your choice here impacts not just movies but stills also.

AF Range Limiter

In this option, you can increase autofocus speed by reducing the focal distances the camera searches for focus.

- **Menu > AF/MF > AF Range Limiter.**

Touch Screen Mode

This is the area where you can set the touch screen's autofocusing operating mode. The menu duplicates the modes that can be selected for still and video photography by using the **Touch Screen icon**. You only need to use this menu if the LCD Touch screen icon is disabled.

- **Menu > AF/MF > Touch screen mode**

Focus Check Lock

This option helps you to remain in focus check while shooting video or not.

- **Menu > AF/MF > Focus Check Lock**

Audio Setting

This menu sheds more light on the various settings for audio.

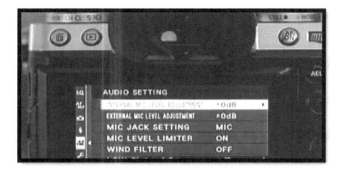

Internal Mic Level Adjustment

This option helps to modify the audio recording levels for the in-built microphone.

There are three options here; Auto, Manual, and Off.
- **Auto**: The camera tries to adjust the audio. This might be great for quick clips or informal filming, but if you want to use the built-in microphone for audio, it might produce "automatic" results that aren't good enough to use.
- **Manual**: You can change the audio recording levels before or during the recording process with just a single press of the function button if you assign this option to one of the 25 available audio levels. It's crucial to remember that the function button is inactive until the movie mode is selected.
- **Off:** This is used to mute the microphone.

It will switch to regulate audio levels for the external mic if you attach an external microphone into the 3.5mm mic socket on the camera and then activate this setting from the Q-Menu or an Fn button.

External Mic Level Adjustment

Just as the name implies, this option helps to modify the audio recording levels for an external microphone plugged into the 3-5mm mic socket.

- **Menu >Audio setting > External Mic Level Adjustment**

Make sure you choose the right option for the microphone that is currently in use if you plan to use these two options to adjust the microphone's volume. Unlike when you press the Fn button or activate the Q-Menu, it does not switch on its own.

Mic Jack Setting

This helps to indicate if an audio source plugged into the jack is a microphone or line in from a piece of different audio equipment.

- **Menu > Microphone > Mic Jack Setting**.

Mic Level Limiter

This option helps to prevent audio clipping for signals outside the range of the mic. It is intended to serve as a line limiter if the microphone distorts as a result of excessive levels. This will try to stop audio clipping if you set the audio recording level too high. The same holds for unexpectedly or exceptionally high inputs. The limiter's cut-in point cannot be adjusted.

- **Menu > Audio setting > Mic Level Limiter**

Wind Filter

This option helps to enable the reduction of wind noise. Given that low frequencies (80-237 Hz) are what wind noise typically produces, it is possible to electronically remove the majority of wind noise from recorded audio. Not only will using an external microphone with a windscreen cut down on wind noise, but it will also lessen popping "p" and "b" sounds. However, if you don't have access to such tools, you might be able to finish the task by using the wind noise feature. Additionally, it eliminates low-frequency sounds that you may want to record, so use it carefully and conduct a test before using it. However, you should not rely on the speaker that is included inside the camera to convince you of the sound quality. Make sure that the headphones you use are suitable for the volume of recording that you intend to capture.

Low Cut Filter

This option helps with the filtering of low-frequency noise for video recording. This filter is also referred to as a bass-cut or high-pass filter because it lets sounds that have frequencies higher than the cut-off point. In this way, it is commonly used to protect electronic circuits from radio or DC noise.

- **Menu > Microphone > Low Cut Filter**

Keeping an eye on the audio meter for the microphone will often reveal the presence of this noise. If it is bouncing without any intended subject input, then you should consider turning on this low-cut filter to clean it up and cut the low frequencies. This will clean it up and remove the low frequencies.

Headphone Volume

This option helps to modify the volume of the headphone. The X-T5 has a USB-C connector, so you can use the included converter to connect headphones to the port and monitor audio while recording. You can use this menu item to adjust the volume. Zero mutes the volume totally, adjustments are usually between 1 and 10.

(Movie) Time Code Setting

This menu reveals the various configurations for time as regards movies.

- **Menu > Time Code Setting**

Time Code Display

Timecodes allow you to precisely reference any moment in audio or video recordings by synchronizing a timing signal that is supplied through cable or GPS. Either format can be used for this. Several cameras spread across the globe can be perfectly synchronized thanks to the Global Positioning System (GPS). When set to ON, it displays the time codes while the movie is being recorded and played back.

- **Menu > Time Code Display**

Start Time Setting

This option helps with the selection of a method to configure the timecode starting time. There are three ways to configure the time code in XT5; manual, current time, and reset.

- **Menu > Timecode > Start Time Setting**.

Count-Up Setting

This option helps to choose when the time code should start running be it from when it is started or during actual video shooting.

- **Rec Run**: Just count the time code as you complete the recording. An adequate amount for a simple movie set with a small number of manually synchronized devices between takes.
- **Free Run**: All you have to do is monitor the time code as the recording is being made. Enough for a basic film shoot with a limited number of manually synchronized devices between shots.
- **Menu > Time code > Count-up Setting**

Drop Frame

This option helps to ensure that the timecodes are kept synchronized at 59.94 and 29.97p.

- **Menu > Timecode > Drop Frame**

HDMI Time Code Output

Here you can send the timecodes to external HDMI devices.

- **Menu > Time code > HDMI Time Code Output**

Exercise

1. Configure the movie setting on your camera.
2. Configure the movie image quality setting on your device.
3. Configure the Movie AF/MF settings.
4. Configure the Audio setting of your device.
5. Make necessary adjustments to the movie time code configuration on your device.

CHAPTER 15

THE SETUP MENUS

In this chapter, you will learn about the settings that are required of you to get the setup menu up and rolling. When you click on a menu item in the Setup Menu, a submenu that contains options that are relevant to that item will open. Consider each of these as a top-level setup menu that also has its menu if that helps clarify things for you. Some of these only have one page of configuration options, while others have more.

User Setting

This option opens a two-page menu of configurations that range from sensor cleaning to battery age, etc.

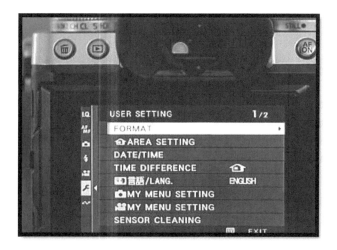

- **Menu > User Setting**

Format

This option helps to format memory cards so they can be effectively used with the camera. A memory card is a compact data storage device that a variety of electronic devices can read and write information to and from. Memory cards are typically flash memory cards. For this to take place, things need to be "structured," which is synonymous with "formatted." This is analogous to the process of establishing a system of filing for documents or a parts catalog for inventory.

However, not every form of storage media is perfect. Imagine a music CD or movie DVD that has some scratches on it. Only the portions that were damaged are unusable; the rest of the CD most likely still functions normally. SD cards are comparable in certain ways. You should not keep photographs in those locations since certain components of them can, on occasion, develop faults; therefore, you must avoid doing so.

- **Menu > Setting > User Setting > Format**

Formatting a card does the following to the card;
- Sets up the structure for data to be stored on the card.
- Create a catalog to know the location of the exact file.
- It erases any previous catalog and data saved on the card
- Locates defective parts of the card that will no longer store data and puts that information in the catalog also.

The protection settings for "Protected" photos are deleted when a memory card is formatted. The majority of people usually use it because, in actuality, formatting the card is a fairly easy way to remove everything it contains, including any password-protected photographs.

Area Setting

This option helps to configure the time zone on a map and also set daylight savings options.
- **Menu > Settings > User Setting > Area Setting**
- **Area Setting:** scroll to either the right or left to choose your time zone on the map.
- **Daylight Savings**: alter appropriately with just some clicks. Helps to save modifying time on the camera.

Date/Time

This option helps to configure a date, time, and date format for your camera. The date and time are also always recorded anytime you shoot an image.

- **Menu > Setting > User Setting > Date/time**

Time Difference

This option allows you to select a date and time for a location outside of your usual (Home) time zone that is in the "Local" format. You'll find this useful if you travel frequently. Even though the device lacks an integrated GPS, you can still set a "Local" time zone that differs from your "Home" time zone.

- To accomplish this, select **"Local" and then press the OK button**. This will take you to a menu where you may adjust the offset amount of hours and minutes to reflect the time difference between your current location and the location you are traveling to.

To make it as failsafe as possible, the time and date at the top of the screen (next to the emblem of an airplane) will change to reflect whatever you have set it to. A yellow airplane icon and a "Local" time and date display will briefly appear over the top of your screen when you turn on the camera. It is probably meant to be a subtle reminder that you are on the road. Additionally, just to remind you to go back **(MENU > Settings > User Setting > Time Difference > Home)**, as there will be additional explanations needed if you don't. After three seconds, this will vanish to free up your vision of the clutter.

Language

In this option, you will be able to choose the language to operate your camera in.

- **Menu > Setting > User Setting > Language**

My Menu Settings

In this option, you can choose items for the MY Menu for stills shooting.

- **Menu > Setting > User Setting > My Menu Setting**

My Menu Setting (Movie)

In this option, you get to choose items for the MY Menu for movies.

- **Menu > Setting > User Setting > My Menu Setting**

Sensor Cleaning

Here, you get to choose when the camera adds sensor cleaning.

- **Menu > Setting > User Setting > Sensor Cleaning**

Battery Age

This is quite a profound and unique option. It helps to show the age of the battery which is usually between 0 and 4.

The higher the number the older your batter.

- **Menu > Setting > User Setting > Battery Age**

Reset

If something goes wrong, or if you can't remember what you altered that caused your camera to start behaving strangely,
- Select the Reset option (Stills, Movie, Set-Up, or INITIALIZE) that matches the mode you are currently in. It's great that, based on the appearance of the problem, you can choose either one or the other. Regardless of the approach you take, this error cannot be made by accident. It is necessary to either select "Cancel" or confirm your menu choice. When you execute the reset, the relevant settings are returned to their initial factory defaults.
- **Menu > Setting > User Setting > Reset**

Sound Setting

In this option, you get to modify the various sound settings.

- **Menu > Setting > Sound Setting**

AF Beep Volume

Here you get to modify the volume of the sound made when the camera gets autofocus locked in AF-S mode.

- **Menu > Setting > Sound Setting > AF Beep Volume**

This is the accessory for you if you enjoy the sound of a chirp whenever the camera autofocuses. You can choose to turn off the focus chirp, but if you do, you'll see a tiny green dot in the viewfinders' lower left corner. This dot only turns green all the way when the AF-S focus lock is locked in. The volume may be too loud for your ears, even at the lowest setting.

Self-Timer Beep Volume

In this opinion, you will be able to modify the volume of the beep played right before the shutter release while the Self-Timer shooting is ongoing.

- **Menu > Setting > Sound Setting > Self-Timer**

Operational Vol. (Volume)

This option modifies the volume of camera controls just like tapping the button when navigating through menus.

- **Menu > Setting > Sound Setting > Operational Volume**

Rec Start/Stop Volume

With this option, you can configure the volume at the start and end of the movie recording.

- **Menu > Setting Sound Setting > Rec Start/Stop Volume**

MS EF Electronic Shutter Sound

In this option, you get to modify the volume of the shutter release volume when making use of the front-curtain shutter. The sound will be completely replaced by the sound of the mechanical shutter if you turn it down all the way. To be sure that you have taken a picture when you want to check later, you might want to turn this on in a busy situation, especially if you are using the electronic shutter.

- **Menu > Setting > Sound Setting > MS EF Electronic Shutter Sound**

ES Electronic Shutter Volume

Here you get to choose the shutter release volume when making use of the electronic shutter.

- **Menu > Setting > Sound Setting > ES Electronic Shutter Volume**

ES Electronic Shutter Sound

Here you get to choose the shutter release sound when making use of the Electronic Shutter.

- Menu > Setting > Sound Setting > ES Electronic Shutter Sound

Playback Volume

Adjusts the amount of audio output during playback of movies captured in-camera. This device uses the built-in speaker of the camera, which is located on the underside of the camera body and resembles many tiny holes, to control how loud movies are played back. A scale is used to depict the range, with "0" denoting silence. There isn't any connection between any other camera sounds and the playback volume.

- Menu > Setting > Sound Setting > Playback Volume

This does the same task as pressing the **OK button** during the playback of a movie (whether the movie is now playing or has been paused).

Screen Setup (Setting)

The third sub-menu under Setup is called Screen Setup. Make adjustments to the display and screen settings.

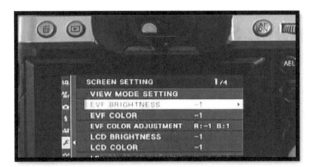

- Menu > Setting > Screen Set-Up.

View Mode Setting

Here you get to modify the settings for the IR sensor control over EVF and LCD viewing modes for both shooting as well as playback.

- **Menu > Setting > Screen Set-up > View Mode Setting**

EVF Brightness

In this option, you can modify the EVF brightness from -7 to +5, or let the camera have control of this. The brightness of the LCD and the electronic viewfinder (EVF) can be individually changed. This is a setting that only impacts the EVF or electronic viewfinder. You will see instructions to Check the Finder if you view the LCD and choose "manual" as the mode of operation. All you have to do to make a change is select the "Manual" mode and, when prompted, look through the viewfinder.

- **Menu > Setting > Screen Set-up > EVF Brightness**

EVF Color Adjustment

This option helps to modify the saturation of the EVF.

- **Menu > Setting > Screen Set-Up > EVF Color**

Fujifilm claims that this is done to adjust the electronic viewfinder's (EVF) saturation. As such, adjusting this will cause the color balance shown in your viewfinder to change. You can watch what happens by adjusting the parameters while focusing on a color wheel or color chart. There is a noticeable shift in the ratio as one navigates the available options.

LCD Brightness

In this option, you will be able to modify the LCD screen brightness from -5 to + 5. Note that there is no Auto setting for LCD brightness.

- **Menu > Setting > Screen Set-Up > LCD Brightness**

If the EVF/LCD Brightness setting has already been assigned to the Q-Menu, you can adjust the LCD brightness by just selecting it and then adjusting it with your touch screen or by turning the command dial on the back. Set **your eye to the viewfinder**, and while keeping it there, turn the command dial on the back of the camera. There is also an "Auto" option available.

LCD Color

Both the LCD and the EVF can have their color (saturation) independently adjusted. Many people will never experience the desire to do this. However, it can be very difficult to deal with White Balance issues if your LCD screen—what Fujifilm calls the monitor—is inaccurate.

- **Menu > Setting > Screen Set-Up > LCD Color**

LCD Color Adjustment

In this option you will be able to modify the color of the EVF display.
- **Menu > Setting > Screen Set-Up > LCD Color Adjustment**

Image Display

With digital cameras, you can quickly adjust the exposure and composition of your images thanks to their quick feedback. To view the captured image, you will need to physically move the camera because this function can only be played back on the LCD of many cameras. With the X-T5, this is not the case. With the electronic viewfinder (EVF), you can quickly review the image you just took without taking your eye off of the viewfinder. If you happen to have this option set to anything other than "Off," the image will playback in the finder that you are now employing, be it the electronic viewfinder (EVF) or the LCD.

Eye Sensor

The capture will show up on the finder that you are currently using, whether it is the LCD or the EVF if you use the View Mode button to select this view mode. You can switch between the two, and depending on your proximity to the infrared eye sensor by the viewfinder, the camera will automatically present the image to you on either of the two displays. If you want to end image playback and go back to shooting mode at any point, you can do so by **pressing the shutter button halfway**.

Display Time

The X-T5 can play back the most recent image that was captured for either half a second (0.5 sec), one and a half seconds (1.5 sec), or constantly up until you push the shutter button. This is a useful tool for getting quick answers on things like figuring out if someone had their eyes closed. Even at 1.5 seconds, though, you should be focused on what you are looking for in your shot because, depending on how quickly you need to take the next picture, a second and a half can pass by quickly. You had better pay attention to what you are looking for in your image, even at 1.5 seconds.

Eye Sensor + LCD Image Display

If you are using this view mode, the capture will not be displayed in the electronic viewfinder (EVF); but, if you draw back, it will display on the LCD. Once you have your eye back on the electronic viewfinder (EVF), you will be back in shooting mode. In certain shooting modes, there might be a small delay when you use the Image Display function before the most recent image you took shows up on the screen. The shooting settings you select will determine how long this delay lasts. Regretfully, you cannot force the camera to ignore the Image Display playback and take a new picture by simply pressing the **shutter button.**

Autorotate Displays

In this option, shooting data modifies orientation in displays to become a match for camera orientation. The data is aligned so that the text appears in the correct orientation when shooting in landscape orientation (wide). Almost all other cameras stay exactly where they are when you change the camera to a portrait (tall) position; you've just grown used to reading everything upside down. However, when you change the camera to landscape orientation, everything flips. Nevertheless, the EVF and LCD screens on the X-T5 can automatically rotate this data for you. Turning "Off" keeps the information in the location you are used to seeing it in.

*   **Menu > Setting > Screen Set-Up > Autorotate Displays**

Preview Exposure & WB in Manual Mode

In manual exposure mode, this option provides a preview of the exposure and/or the white balance.

*   **Menu > Setting > Screen Set-Up > Preview Exp./WB in Manual Mode**

Preview Exp. /WB

Previews of exposure and white balance are displayed on the screen. The viewfinder shows the effects of any WB settings you have applied as well as a signal indicating whether the exposure settings you have chosen have resulted in an overexposed or underexposed composition. The LCD is most visible when it is either extremely light or extremely black. The camera always considers the exposure setting that is "perfect"; this can be found by utilizing the histogram, which is the small exposure indicator gauge on the left side of the screen. It will become evident very quickly that the WB is also being previewed when you take an anomalous WB into account.

Preview WB

This is limited to WB previews. The exposure is not previewed. Verification of this requires minimal work. You'll notice that the WB shifts to match your preset, but the exposure does not if you adjust the white balance or exposure too much. You will be able to see the WB of modeling or ambient lights, as well as the impact of colored reflectors, without worrying about exposure issues. Preview exposure and white balance in Manual Mode can be assigned to a Function button for convenient access. There is something you may want to consider if you are shooting in a studio with modeling lights or manual flash. Though you can still place it in the MY Menu, you won't be able to attach it to the Q-Menu.

Natural Live View

In this option, you can preview the effects of film Sims, WB, etc as they will be added to the images you capture, or seen in an untouched view.

- **Menu > Setting > Screen Set-Up > Natural Live View**

You can preview the effects of various settings, such as color, tone, sharpening, film simulations, white balance, and others, on the photos you shoot by adjusting this setting. In nearly all cases, you should turn this off because doing so will guarantee that you are seeing the effects of your settings rather than the "natural view". Still, there's a benefit to having it activated. Not surprisingly, you won't see these cumulative impacts in the finders while they are ON. You may want to turn this on when shooting in challenging lighting conditions, such as shadows because some adjustments mask what's happening in those areas (like backlighting). This is especially true if you are shooting RAW+JPEG/HEIF and intend to use the RAW files later.

Focus Scale Units

This is a matter of taste, and in a time crunch, you should base your decision on what seems the most sensible to you. The focus distance indicator tells you the width of your depth of field in addition to the distance at which your lens is focused. The depth (measured in feet or meters) that is in focus around your focus point is how this information is expressed. The locked focus distance is indicated by the white line that passes through the center of the blue envelope on the scale, which represents the depth of field.

- **Menu > Setting > Screen Set-Up > Focus Scale Units**

Aperture Unit for Cinema Lens

The aperture can be shown as either t-numbers or f-numbers when using MKX cine lenses. You may be surprised to learn that apertures in cine lenses are expressed in t-stops instead of f-stops. Every lens has some amount of light loss when used, and this loss varies depending on the particular lens. T-stops are used by the motion picture industry to standardize lens exposure.

- **Menu > Setting > Screen Set-Up > Aperture Unit for Cinema Lens**

T-Stop

T-numbers account for both lens transmittance and aperture to provide more accurate exposure calculations. One lens's T Number and another lens's T Number can be used interchangeably. This is important because visuals, or video frames, are viewed quickly one after the other, and even minute changes in exposure can be very noticeable to the viewer.

F-Stop

When taking still photos, this setting is used. It is a common misconception that lenses have a 100% transmittance, but this is never the case. This means that using the same aperture (f-stop) setting on one lens with another will usually result in a different exposure. Photographers are very used to thinking this way, and they know that an aperture is not going to produce an exposure that is the same with every lens.

Location Info

Shows the location information if it was taken from a smartphone as the shot was being taken. If this is turned on and geotagging was turned on when the image was recorded, then you will be able to view the geotagging location data for the image when it is played back in play-back mode if both of these conditions are met. You won't see a screen with a lovely map and a pin identifying the spot where the image was shot because that's not how this works. Instead, there will be geotagging of the data.

Q-Menu Background (Stills & Movie)

This option helps to alter the Q menu background from Black, to Transparent for stills shooting alone.

- **Menu > Setting > Button/Dial Setting > Q Menu Background**

Button/Dial Setting

In this menu, you can modify various buttons, dial as well as touch settings.

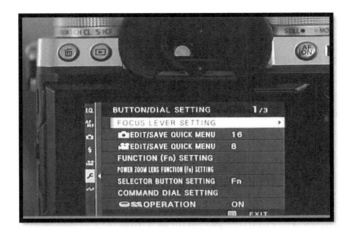

- Menu > Settings > Button/Dial Setting

Function (Fn) Setting

Almost eighty different functions, including the NO setting, can be accessed by reassigning each of the function buttons, the four swipe motions, the AE-L and AF-On buttons, the Q button, View Mode, and the back dial press. It's noteworthy that the X-T5 allows you to modify the functions of the Q button, the rear command dial press, and the AF-On button.

- Menu > Settings > Button/Dial Setting > Function (Fn) Setting

Power Zoom Lens Function (Fn) Setting

You can adjust the Function button settings on certain power zoom lenses. The default options are associated with the Zoom and focus ring controls. On the other hand, the Fn button on the power zoom lens can be assigned to most camera functions that can be assigned to regular function buttons.

- Menu > Setting > Button/ Dial Setting > Power Zoom Lens Function (Fn) Setting

Selector Button Setting

You can adjust the Function button settings on certain power zoom lenses. The default options are associated with the Zoom and focus ring controls. On the other hand, the Fn button on the power zoom lens can be assigned to most camera functions that can be assigned to regular function buttons.

- Menu > Setting > Button/Dial Setting > Selector Button Setting

Command Dial Setting

In this option, you will be able to select how front and rear command dials function for shooting stills.

- **Menu > Setting > Button/Dial Setting > Command Dial Setting**

The functions that the front command dial controls can be altered by pressing the front dial. And that's possibly part of the reason this configuration seems challenging. By selecting the functions of each of these "press" options, you can set and then arrange the three controls that appear on the front dial when you press the dial while shooting. There are three of these "press" options, denoted as Front Command Dial 1, 2, and 3.

S.S Operation

In this option, you will be able to fine-tune the shutter speed with a command dial. Changing the shutter speed with the shutter speed dial is in full stop increments. This setting should be enabled for finer control.

- **Menu > Setting > Button/Dial Setting > S.S Operation**

Command Dial Direction

This option helps with changing the direction of the dial. Right, can be used to increase the value or left to decrease it. You are at liberty to configure this as you want.

- **Menu > Setting > Button/Dial Setting > Command Dial Direction**

Shutter AF (Back Button Focus)

You can select whether the camera should autofocus in AF-S, continuously focus in AF-C, or not focus at all with this option. The shutter button must be pressed halfway. Since cameras can autofocus, ON is frequently used. OFF separates the shutter button from the autofocus. The term "back button focus" refers to the fact that the shutter button is only used to fire the shutter and lock the exposure; a separate button on the back of the camera is used to lock the focus. To avoid holding the shutter button during focus-recompose shots or to stop the camera from attempting autofocus when they want to fire the shutter, many photographers prefer to decouple autofocus from the shutter button. There are many different viewpoints on this topic, so if you do some research online, you might find a wide range of opinions.

- **Menu > Settings > Button/Dial Setting > Shutter AF**

Shutter AE

Here you get to decide if the camera should lock exposure or not when the shutter button is pressed halfway.

Exposure for Still Image Shots

Turning off this feature will separate AE-Lock from the shutter release button for still images, meaning that exposure will only be locked when the shutter is fired, not when you partially press the shutter. You can always use the AE-L button to lock the AE if you decide at any point that you would like to.

Burst Shooting (Exposure between shots)

There is a very good reason to switch off burst mode, also called continuous shooting, if you are using it. The camera can adjust the exposure between each burst mode photo if you turn it OFF. If you activate this feature, the exposure will be fixed at the start of the sequence. Whether or not you use this feature depends on how much light is available at the moment of the burst shot. In the unlikely event that things drastically improve, going with this course of action would probably be wise.
  • **Menu > Setting > Button/Dial Setting > Shoot Without Lens**

Shoot Without Lens

In this option, you can enable firing the shutter when the camera doesn't know there is a lens. This can happen anytime even when there is a lens.
  • **Menu > Setting > Button/Dial Setting > Shoot Without Lens**

Shoot Without Card

This is where you can select whether a memory card needs to be present for you to shoot. The shutter won't operate if this option is disabled. This can act as a check to prevent firing indefinitely even in the absence of a card.
  • **Menu > Setting > Button/Dial Setting > Shooting Without Card**

AE/AF-Lock Mode

In this option, you can specify if the AF On and the AE-L buttons act as toggles or if you need to hold them to be able to make use of them.
  • **Menu > Setting > Button/ Dial Setting > AE/AF Lock Mode**

AWB-Lock Mode

Decides if an assigned AWB-Lock Fn button can be used as a toggle (switch) or if the AWB needs to be held down (pressed) to be momentarily locked. Now, by using the Fn button that has been assigned to the function, you can lock the WB at any time while using Auto White Balance. With this option, you can decide whether to hold down the button while working or activate it with a quick push. Like with the previous setting, toggle mode is my favorite way to turn the AWB on/off switch.

- **Menu > Setting > Button/Dial Setting > AWB-Lock Mode**

Aperture Ring Setting (A)

In this option, you can choose if you would like to soft-switch aperture when the lens is on A or not. This functions pretty much in the same way as gently switching between ISO settings. After setting the lens aperture to the "A" position, move it to the "Command" position, and finally select an option from the front command dial to adjust the aperture. Now, the dial can be rotated to adjust the aperture.

- **Menu > Setting > Button/Dial Setting > Aperture Ring Setting (A)**

Aperture Setting

Here you get to indicate how you would like to adjust the aperture on lenses with no aperture ring. This option is usually grayed out unless you are making use of such a lens.

Auto + Manual: this enables shooting with all PASM exposure modes. The other two modes don't do this.
- **P**: when the camera is turned on, this means you are automatically in Program exposure mode, and the camera selects the aperture for you.
- **A**: Rotate the dial on the front of the camera to the left to select an aperture setting. The F/16 (for the 27mm XF) at the bottom of the screen indicates that you are currently shooting in Aperture Priority mode. To choose the desired aperture, keep rolling the dial in the desired direction.
- **M**: Naturally, you will enter the Manual exposure mode and have to manually adjust the shutter speed as well as the aperture if you follow the above instructions AND turn the shutter speed dial away from the A position.
- **S**: If you want to keep the aperture at its default setting, avoid touching the front command dial. You are now in the shutter priority mode; all you need to do is move the shutter speed off of A.
- **Menu > Settings > Button/Dial Setting > Aperture Setting**

FN 1 Button Setting

In this option, you can choose what the Fn 1 button decides to do in the Playback mode.
- **Smartphone Transfer Order**: Choose images for upload to a phone.
- **Wireless Communication**: initiates an immediate wireless connection to control the camera remotely with the use of a smartphone or transfer images.

Touch Screen Setting

In this setting, you can enable or disable the various touch screen modes. OR disable the touchscreen.
- **Touch Screen Setting**: This switch disables the touchscreen, so you can simply flip it off to make the icon on the LCD vanish if you're not using it. Furthermore, this turns off touch in the Q-Menu and during playback—two areas where touch is incredibly useful.
- **Double Tap Setting**: tap the LCD screen while shooting to zoom.
- **T-Fn Touch Function**: here you can enable the touch screen gestures. Acts like 4 more function buttons. Although it works only on the LCD.
- **Touch Zoom**: touch the screen to power zoom lenses.
- **Touch Screen Setting**: This feature allows the touch screen to be used in playback mode. You will likely have the screen open while the media is playing back, so this is a very useful feature to enable.
- **EVF Touch Screen Area Settings (Mouse Mode)**: While keeping one eye on the viewfinder, use the touch controls on the LCD to operate the camera in the same manner as you would on the LCD. Adjust the LCD screen so that it uses this particular area.

Lock

In this option, you can lock all or some buttons and dials when shooting. You can choose to assign this function to a button. Tapping the button will switch on the lock state.

Lock Setting

Choose the controls to lock when you tap the assigned lock function button;
- **Unlock** locks no buttons or dials.
- **All functions**: locks all buttons and dials when you touch the Fn button.
- **Selected Function**: only locks the controls indicated in the next menu item.

Function Selection

If you chose "Selected Function" in the previous menu AND pressed the designated "Lock" Fn button, this option will allow you to indicate which buttons and dials you want to be locked.

Power Management

In this menu, you will learn how you can get the most out of your camera in terms of power and also how you can effectively manage the power so it lasts for the duration of your use.

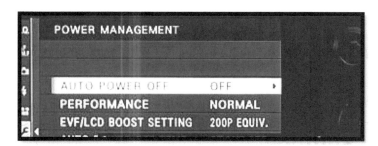

- Menu > Setting > Power Management

Auto Power Off

In this option, the camera standby delays.
- Menu > Settings > Power Management > Auto Power Off

Performance

The performance option has an impact on focus speed, display quality as well as battery. There are three different boost modes: Boost, as its name suggests, elevates all of your important performances; Normal, which has significantly longer battery life but much slower AF times and lower viewfinder refresh rates; Economy is a relatively novel setting. The LCD's performance keeps getting worse, which lengthens the battery's life. Time-lapse photography, astrophotography, manual focus or exposure, strolls to discover a new city, and related pursuits are among its many applications.
- Menu > Setting > Power Management > Performance

EVF/LCD Boost Setting

In this option, you get to configure different EVF performance options when in the Boost mode.

There are four options here;
- **EVF/LCD Low Light Priority**: modifies EVF/LCD to make dark details brighter.
- **EVF/LCD Resolution Priority**: Increase EVF/LCD show resolution to make details much clearer.

- **EVF Frame Rate Priority (100p):** makes use of 1oofps EVF refresh rate to smoothen motion in the EVF.
- **EVF Frame Rate Priority (200p EQUIV):** makes use of the highest EVF refresh rate to smooth motion in the EVF. EVF brightness often drops here.

Auto Power off Temp

This option configures an undefined temperature at which the camera will then go off if it overheats.

- Menu > Settings > Power Management > Auto Power Off Temp

Save Data Settings

In this menu, you will learn about data savings as regards images and movies.

- Menu > Setting > Save Data Set-Up

Frame No. (Frame Number)

This option helps to indicate if the camera resets the file numbering scheme each time you replace memory cards or reformat the one in use. Choose "Continuous" for the Frame Number setting on your camera to instruct it to "Number my files in order until you reach 9,999." This will cause your camera to continue counting until you reach 9,999, no matter how many times you remove or reformat your memory card. When you set this to "Renew," on the other hand, you are instructing the camera to "Start numbering at "1" each time I reformat or insert a new memory card."

- Menu > Settings > Save Data Set-up > Frame No

Edit File Name

This option allows you to activate limited in-camera file naming, which may allow you to assign a unique ID to every picture taken with this camera. Would you like to change the four letters (sRGB) or the three letters (aRGB) that make up each file's unique identity? This is the place where you execute it. It is possible to alter the "names" of either type of file independently because sRGB and aRGB files have different file name formats.

- Menu > Setting >Save Data Set-Up > Edit File Name

When working with sRGB files, you can change the filename by up to four characters. You will need to modify your naming convention to account for shooting in aRGB. In aRBG, you can only alter three of your characters. Any changes you make to a file's name take effect immediately, as you might expect. This may be a little confusing for you if there are still pictures on the memory card that are named differently. As a result, I now incorporate it into my initial setup, which I complete right before I start using the camera to take pictures.

Card Slot Setting (Stills)

You can choose what the camera stores on each memory card when taking still photos with this option. While having two memory cards is convenient, you should also know how to use them effectively when taking pictures.

- **Sequential**: this option means that a second card will only be used to save stills when the first card is filled up.
- **Backup**: this indicates that both cards have saved images. Both files will be saved to both cards when shooting in RAW+JPEG. For the two cards, the folder and file names are identical.
- **Separate**: this means the RAW file saves to card 1, and the JPEG/HEIF to card 2. Since RAW files are larger than either JPEG or HEIF you should make use of this option.

Select Slot (Stills Sequential)

In this, you can choose the memory card the camera records pictures to first if you have chosen the sequential option in the memory card slot setting. This is an action, nothing fancy, just a plain scene. The camera will instantly switch to the selected memory card slot after you've selected one and hit OK. The camera will not start saving pictures to the other card until the currently selected card has reached its maximum capacity and is still operating normally. The currently active card will be highlighted on the screen. This choice becomes unavailable if the "Sequential" option for the preceding Card Slot was NOT selected, or if there is only one card currently installed in the camera.

- **Menu > Setting > Save Data Set-Up > Select Slot**

Select Folder

In this option, you can create or select a memory card folder to save still images. You can create a new folder just for storing stills and movies, or you can select an already-existing folder. You can use the onscreen keyboard that appears when you create a folder to give it a name. This process works the same as it does in the following option.

- **Menu > Setting > Save Data Set-Up > Select Folder**

Copyright Info

The procedure for changing the file name and entering copyright information is fairly similar. You can select symbols and choose between upper and lower case (though there isn't a copyright symbol). Make sure you hit the **SET button** after entering the data.

- **Menu > Settings > Save Data Set-Up > Copyright Info**
- **Enter Author's Info:** Here you will insert the name of the author or photographer.
- **Enter Copyright Info**: Here you will insert the name of the copyright holder which sometimes is the same as the name of the photographer but this is not necessary.
- **Disp Copyright Info**: shows the two copyright entries on a single screen.
- **Delete Copyright Info**: this takes off the copyright info inserted, and it will not record copyright info on later images. It does not erase copyright info from images on the memory card.

Geotagging

You can choose to enable or disable geotagging with this option. Whether or not location data is downloaded and stored in the EXIF data is determined by this option in the Geotagging menu. Your phone must be turned on, the GPS feature activated, and the Fujifilm Camera Remote App active for you to download GPS data from it.

- **Menu > Settings > Save Data Setting > Geotagging**

Exercise

1. Configure the user settings of your device for easy use.
2. Configure the screen setup menu.
3. Configure the button/dial setting.
4. Configure the power management settings of your device.

CHAPTER 16

NETWORK / USB SETTING

This chapter deals with the settings that can be accessed via the Network/ USB Settings Menu. You can reset all the Set-Up options by making use of one of the Set-Up menu items.

- Menu > Settings > User Setting > Reset > Set-Up Reset

Bluetooth/Smartphone Setting

In this option, you can connect the camera to a smartphone. Bluetooth settings for on/Off, Pairing, selecting a device, deleting a pairing, Image Transfer, and geolocation syncing- and more.

Pairing Registration

It is necessary to pair the camera with your phone or another device. Just choose this option, and your device will launch Fujifilm Camera Remote. On the device, select Pairing Registration from the list of options. A maximum of seven devices can be paired. Thus, you can pair them together if you frequently use a phone and a tablet!

Bluetooth On/Off

When the camera is turned on, it will automatically establish a connection with any Bluetooth device that it has previously been paired with. If you do not want to use the Auto Image Transfer feature, you can turn this feature off. That's one less piece of radio equipment to deal with now. Using Bluetooth will make connecting devices easier when using the Fujifilm Camera Remote App.

Auto Image Transfer Order

ON causes all of the photographs that you capture to be marked for transfer automatically as you take them. OFF does not. You still have the opportunity to manually annotate photographs while they are being played back by selecting the Transfer Image to Smartphone function.

Smartphone Location Sync

Here you can sync location and time or location alone and time alone when the camera is connected to your phone.

Airplane Mode

You may turn off Bluetooth, Wi-Fi, and LAN as well as all other wireless connectivity in this mode. Under the "Network/USB" menu, this is the most basic option. All of the radios built into the camera are turned off by pressing the ON button. When turned on, Internet Explorer will prevent connections to Bluetooth, LANs, and wireless networks altogether.

- **Menu > Network/USB > Airplane Mode**

Network Setting

In this menu, you can configure a wireless network connection. When paired with software like Fujifilm X Acquire, the X-T5 uses this wireless network configuration for wireless tethering. The first step is to figure out how the camera connects to your Wi-Fi network so that you can utilize it later on. This is the point at which everything is configured.

- **Menu > Settings > Connection Setting > Network Setting**

Access Point Setting

Here you can simply do an automatic or manual connection of your camera to a wireless network.

Simple Setup

Requires that you have a Wi-Fi router that supports the WPS (push) protocol. If you don't have it or you don't know what it is, this could be a good opportunity to obtain some assistance from a tech support specialist.

Manual Setup

To pick your router,

- Choose **"Select from Network List"** from the list of choices. Make sure you are close to the router when you do this so it can get the most power and become the most popular item on the list. As soon as your camera has finished searching, you will see the list. After choosing the desired router, input the password.

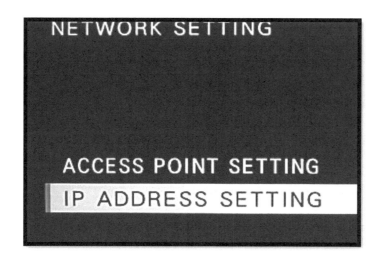

IP Address Setting

To have access to full operation inside of a network, there is a need for you to have an IP address.

Auto

Permit the camera to function within a wireless network by having it automatically receive an IP address from the router.

Manual

Set the camera's IP address, network mask, and gateway address using the camera's manual settings.

Connection Mode

Select an already-established connection or profile. This entails selecting your current camera connection method based on user-generated and in-camera profiles.

- Menu > Network/USB > Connection Mode

USB card Reader

You can transfer the photos from the memory card to a phone or computer that has a USB card reader attached to it.

USB Webcam

You can use your XT5 as a webcam; it has a very good quality for a webcam.

USB Tether Shooting Auto

If you want to take pictures and control the camera from your computer, choose this USB tethering option. The device that is connected to the camera controls it in this mode. Software packages for tethering come in a wide variety. X-Acquire is simple to do. For more expert-looking shots, you can also connect this to a gimbal or a drone.

USB RAW Conv. /Backup Restore

To use the Backup and Restore feature or to perform RAW conversions, you will need to connect your camera to a computer. Even though these two setups are entirely different from one another, they are both USB-connected to computers.

USB Power Supply/ Comm Setting

In this option, you can make use of the USB port to power the camera or use it to exchange data such as transferring images.

- **Menu > Network/USB > Create/Edit Connection Setting**

Information

This shows the MAC address, Bluetooth MAC address, and IP address of the camera when it is connected. All electrical equipment that is networkable is uniquely identified by a MAC address. Two distinct devices' Media Access Control (MAC) addresses can never be the same. Every X-T5 has a unique Media Access Control (MAC) address. This address, sometimes referred to as an identification number, allows Bluetooth or a network to identify devices that seem similar but are kept apart from one another.

This suggests that multiple identical devices can operate under the same network or Bluetooth connection without confusion. You are unable to change the MAC addresses stored on your X-T5, but it is important to be aware of what they are in case you encounter problems with your wireless network or Bluetooth connection.

- **Menu > Network/USB > Information**

Reset Network / USB Setting

Here you can choose to reset all of your wireless connections.

- **Menu > Network/ USB > Reset Network/USB Setting**

Exercise

1. Pair your camera with a smartphone using Bluetooth.
2. Configure the network settings on your device.
3. Rest network and USB settings if need be.

CHAPTER 17

DIGITAL IMAGING TOPICS

In this chapter, we will discuss the advantages of shooting in RAW, and I will also provide some insight into the processing of RAW photographs. If you've been shooting in RAW for a while, you probably already have a process established and are familiar with the effective tools.

An Introduction to RAW

Digital photography makes extensive use of the RAW file format. It captures the information straight out of the camera's image sensor—untouched by compression or editing. It retains maximum information retention and offers more post-processing flexibility when compared to other file formats such as JPEG. RAW files are unprocessed photos that hold all of the information that the camera's image sensor was able to record. This includes details about the brightness, color, and other aspects of the image. The bit depth of the RAW format is usually between 12 and 14 bits, which is greater than the 8-bit depth of JPEG files. This produces a more expansive tonal range. RAW files offer significant advantages to post-processing workflows because they maintain all of the original image data. You can more easily adjust exposure, white balance, contrast, and sharpening during the editing process without appreciably lowering the image's quality. RAW files allow for non-destructive editing, so the original data is preserved and the edits are stored in a different location. To convert RAW files into a format that can be viewed, such as JPEG or TIFF, the files need to be processed with specialized software such as Adobe Camera Raw, Lightroom, or the manufacturer's proprietary RAW converter. During this stage, changes can be made to the properties of the image, such as the exposure, the white balance, and the tone curves.

How Cameras Create JPEGs/HEIFs

As soon as you hit the shutter button, the camera reads data off of the sensor (the RAW data), and then it begins to "develop" the image based on two criteria, which are as follows:

The algorithms that are incorporated into the camera and used to convert RAW data to JPEG or HEIF format, doing "corrections' such as the lens and other adjustments. The JPEG and HEIF settings that you apply use a range of different parameters (e.g., size, advanced filter, film simulation, NR, DR, sharpening, color, grain effect, tone, and so on). This is why a compressed RAW file is much larger than a JPEG or HEIF file, which can be quite small. The reason for this is that the data is being erased. Furthermore, once that data is deleted and the JPEG is saved to the memory card, it can never be retrieved. Consequently, unless you were shooting in RAW + JPEG at the time, there's not much you can do if the outcome of your combined JPEG modifications doesn't, please you. The EXIF data in the RAW file preserves shooting information such as white balance, noise reduction, and other settings that can be applied to the RAW data by certain software. This information is included in the RAW file so that your computer will be able to comprehend what was happening when you took the picture. You are not obligated to allow it to behave in that manner, of course. When developing JPEGs from RAW data on a desktop computer, you have the option of ignoring the EXIF shooting data and re-creating an entirely new white balance, exposure, noise reduction, and other settings.

File Types-RAW, TIF, JPEG, HEIF

It is necessary to compress data to minimize the size of a file. There are two primary methods for accomplishing this goal: either compact a file while maintaining all of its data or remove "bits" that won't be missed. This is the result you get when you compress other files using ZIP or RAR. There is no loss of data at any point. However, when it comes to pictures (and music), both of which contain data that the human eye and brain might not notice is missing, some room for manipulation can be accomplished by choosing to exclude data. This concept refers to file types that are either lossless (retain all data) or lossy (leave out data), depending on whether or not the data is preserved.

RAW

RAW files are lossless, meaning they contain every bit of image data that was captured by the sensor. Even compressed RAW files retain their original quality.

TIFF

Even though taking pictures with your camera won't produce TIF files, you still need to be aware of this. Despite requiring massive file sizes (often much bigger than those required for RAW files), TIFF is a lossless file compression format that yields high-quality photos. It is advised to save images in TIFF format if you wish to keep them while they are being processed. By doing this, the picture data will be protected from loss.

JPEG

Picture formats in the JPG format are widely used. It produces files that are relatively small in size, but they are lossy—that is, to meet the compression target, it often replaces actual image data with more "average" data, discarding actual image data. This will only be used to dump image data that is difficult for the human eye to perceive. But as we have all seen this in action, we also know that it often goes much further than we would have liked it to.

HEIF

(High-Efficiency Image Format) is a more recent format that is similar to JPEG. Its foundation is essentially video compression using HEVC or H.265; this more modern method allows it to produce higher quality files with smaller file sizes (than JPEG). Compared to image files, JPG files can be encoded and decoded considerably faster. With the same or better image quality than JPEG, HEIF generates images with about half the file size. Beyond this, there's a lot more to it, like picture transparency, 16-bit color, and in-image edits like rotation and cropping that preserve the original image's appearance. Interoperability is a SINGLE drawback. At present time, files are not capable of being uniformly decoded by the software or devices used as end viewers. When native viewing is supported by web browsers, though, you will know that it is finally here.

JPG Artifacts

You would consider JPEG to be a standard, and in a sense, it is. But not all JPEGs are equal. As it turns out, some are more equal than others! The "standard" that JPEG adheres to does not specify how much compression should be applied to an image, which is why this occurs. That choice is up to whoever is using the product in the end. If you have ever handled JPEG photographs on a personal computer, you will be familiar with the "Quality" option that appears when you save the file. You are now deliberating on the quantity of data to be discarded at this stage. If you use the "low quality" preset, the file will, as expected, be of a considerably smaller size. The X-T5 has two different settings for JPEG Image Quality: Fine and Normal. Additionally, two levels of RAW compression need to be taken into consideration. Generally speaking, each uncompressed RAW picture occupies twice as much memory card storage as a lossless RAW and three times as much as a compressed RAW. Furthermore, for every uncompressed RAW file you shoot, you can choose to save 4 Normal JPEG/HEIF files or 6 Fine JPEG/HEIF files.

RAW Processing

Now you are ready to launch RAW processing. Below are titbits you need to learn about processing RAW images;

RAW Conversion

The term "RAW conversion" refers to the process of converting RAW image files, which are those that are acquired by a camera, into forms that may be viewed and edited, such as JPEG or TIFF. It is necessary to convert RAW files to properly bring out their full potential and make them appropriate for viewing and editing since RAW files include image data that has not been processed.

Noise Reduction

The majority of RAW converter software has a noise reduction feature. In addition, there are independent applications that offer good noise reduction as well, such as Topaz Denoise, Noise ware, and NeatImage, all of which also have plugins for Photoshop and Lightroom.

- Highlight the **RAW file Converter EX noise reduction pane**. Select **a noise preset from the dropdown** and then choose **the Noise Reduction icon** to further tweak this setting.

Sharpness

Sharpness increases in a direct proportion to the amount of noise eliminated. Sharpening will typically cause noise levels to rise. The superior sharpening techniques of NeatImage partially mitigates this issue.

Software Options

To convert RAW files, you will need software that can process RAW data. There is a large range of software available, including software from third parties (like Adobe Camera Raw, Capture One, or DxO PhotoLab) and software from the manufacturer (like Canon Digital Photo Professional or Nikon Capture NX-D). These photo-editing software programs provide an array of tools and features that can be applied to alter different aspects of the image and produce the desired outcome.

Fujifilm X RAW Studio

A RAW File Converter can be used to process photos on a computer, but the camera's built-in RAW engine can now be used to process RAW files on a computer. This indicates that a computer will be needed to perform the processing; it won't happen on your computer directly. With this method, post-processing is done using the camera's processor and pre-installed software, giving the impression that the work was completed at the time of shooting. You can either process multiple photos at once or convert one image at a time. In the list of benefits, quickness and the same high-quality images produced by the camera are both mentioned. You can visit the Fujifilm website to download this software.

Tone Curves

Tone curves are a potent tool found in image editing software that can be used to alter both the contrast and tonal range of an image. They make it possible to precisely control how the brightness values of various tones are distributed throughout the image, from the highlights to the shadows. Using tone curves, which let you adjust the image's overall tone, increase contrast, and more, you can create a particular look or feel in your photos. Tone curve adjustments can significantly affect the overall mood, contrast, and tonal balance of your photos. The distribution of brightness values is entirely within your control. By adjusting the curve to your preferred specifications, you can match your creative vision or create a specific style.

S-Curve-Adss Contrast

An S-curve is a type of tone curve alteration that is commonly applied to the curve to increase the contrast in an image. By reshaping the tone curve into an S, you can increase the brightness of the highlights and shadows on the spot. This gives you the option to either greatly compress or maintain the mid-tones at the same brightness level. This adjustment can add depth and impact to the image by enhancing the contrast between the image's light and dark areas. The combination of brightened highlights, deepened shadows, and tweaked mid-tones creates a visually pleasing contrast that gives the image more depth and dimension. The S-curve adjustment can be very helpful when applied to images that lack contrast or when you want to add a sense of drama and impact. The x-axis shows the input tone. The y-axis shows what will happen to a particular tone when you move the curve either up or down.

Brightening Curve

The brightening curve is a relatively straightforward one. If you bring both the highlights and the shadows up, you will notice that your image has gained brightness.

Darkening Curve

This is just the opposite of the brightening curve. Bring the highlights and shadows down to darken the curve.

Exercise

1. Create JPEGS and HEIFs with the use of your camera.
2. Explore the various RAW processing options in the camera.
3. Explore the tone curve settings on your device.

CHAPTER 18

TECH TOPICS

In this chapter, you will learn about some relational tech topics, you can check them through when you are quite free.

The Sensor

The Fujifilm X-T5 has Fujifilm's fifth iteration of the X-Trans sensor as its primary imaging component. This 5th generation X-Trans BSI CMOS 5 HR (40MP) sensor may not have the same burst shooting rates as the X-H2s, but it was designed with an emphasis on resolution. Despite this, it still offers extremely respectable shooting speeds overall.

CMOS & BSI

A backside illuminated (BSI) sensor is something that was more recently introduced by Fujifilm. The advantage of BSI technology is greater performance in low-light conditions, as well as improved dynamic range and reduced noise. In practical terms, this results in a native ISO that is 125 stops lower. The ability of CMOS sensors to execute a variety of activities, like autofocus and noise reduction, directly on the sensor contributes to the speed with which the camera can function.

Phase Detect AF

It is not sufficient to summarize the features of these new sensors in terms of speed, resolution, and low-light performance. The entire sensor is effectively covered by the pixel array used for phase detection. The benefit is that you can use the quicker and more accurate PDAF (Phase Detect) focus instead of the CDAF (Contrast Detect) focus to concentrate on any area of the composition. The low light limit of the PDAF has been raised dramatically, from -1EV in the early sensors to -7EV! This implies that even in environments with lower illumination levels, focusing on low light with PDAF is more accurate than it has ever been.

The most evident benefit of all of this is the faster autofocus, which comes in particularly handy in intriguing low-light and low-contrast situations. All 425 focus points on the X-T5's 40MP X-Trans CMOS 5 HR BSI sensor and the X-H2s's 26MP X-Trans CMOS 5 HS BSI sensor are phase-detect and can be selected directly. This means that you may quickly and accurately autofocus wherever you want within a composition. Additionally, this results in significant improvements to the tracking of the eye, face, and subject.

The X-Processor 5

The amount of processing power available in cameras continues to rise (at what appears to be an almost exponential rate), just as it does in all other types of personal computing. Along with this speed comes the capability to add new 'features,' which are new methods of processing raw data to optimize it for the sensor and lenses on the camera. And to perform some complex post-processing maneuvers in-camera to achieve fantastic outcomes. The X-T5 comes equipped with the brand-new X-Processor 5, which has a processing speed that is twice as fast as the X-Processor 4 found in the X-T4!

14-bit RAW

In 2008, Nikon debuted 14-bit imaging, however, many consumers had trouble noticing any difference in the quality of their photographs after making the switch. Perhaps you can relate to this as well. The only time you are very likely to notice it is if you have underexposed the image by a significant amount and are fervently hoping to recover detail from the shadows. In this scenario, you are likely to notice it. The photographs can resist significantly more severe editing; but you won't be able to tell the difference on a standard computer monitor or printer because these devices are unable to portray the gradations of tone that are present in the original photograph.

Memory Cards

The X-T5 contains what is known as a high-speed "memory buffer" that is designed to store images after they have been taken and before they are written to an SD card. This was done to account for the aforementioned limitation. The amount of space available in this camera's internal buffer plays a key influence in determining how many photographs may be taken in a row without the camera slowing down or coming to a complete halt while it writes the pictures to the memory card. In contrast to the buffer of the X-H2(s), which can save up to 1000 shots at 15 fps, the X-T5 can only store 119 JPEG frames at 15 fps or 39 compressed RAW frames. Neither of these numbers is particularly impressive.

Fujifilm X-Acquire -Tethered Shooting and Settings Backup

Tethering is typically utilized by professionals filming in controlled environments, and professionals are already aware of the method of tethering. Tethering is employed by professionals. But there are some reasons why you would wish to tether, and there is most certainly a solid reason to utilize the program to back up or restore the settings on your camera.

Settings Backup and Restore

In this section, you will be able to back up and restore all camera settings;
- In **Menu > Network / USB > Connection Mode choose USB RAW Conv/Backup Restore**.
- Connect the camera to the PC with a USB cable.
- Power up the camera. The LED blinks to display the connection.
- Start X-Acquire; which shows in the taskbar of the computer.
- Click twice on the icon to see the various options and also do a backup.
- Exit X-Acquire when complete. Switch off the camera.

Connecting Images In-Camera

If you currently have X-T5 RAW photos saved on your computer, you can also use this software to convert them by using the processing engine built into the camera. Nevertheless, you can now process multiple photos over USB thanks to this new feature. According to Fujifilm, this is done for speed reasons because the CPU in a camera can complete a task faster than the processor in a computer.

Video Editing Software

Below are certain software that can be used to edit movies as cameras do not come with software for this purpose;
The software you should use to create full-length feature films with your editing program is Adobe Premiere Pro or Avid Media Composer. There are many more packages available in addition to these, including Cyberlink Powerdirector, Nero Platinum, Pinnacle Studio, and Corel VideoStudio Pro. For users of Mac computers, there are Adobe Premiere Elements and Apple Final Cut Pro. Linux users have two options: Lightworks and OpenShot. Many companies sell "stripped-down" versions of their software that still include some of the most helpful features for professionals. For example, Movie Studio from Magix costs $130, while Premiere Elements from Adobe and Composer First from Avid Media cost between $70 and $130. These packages are much simpler to use even though the Pro versions have more features and require a higher level of expertise.

Exercise

1. Configure the Sensor on your camera.
2. What is the function of the X-processor?
3. Mention 3 software that can be used for video editing.

Wrap up

The Fujifilm X-T5 is without a doubt an excellent camera. It is also an affordable price for a camera that competes with high-end cameras from other manufacturers that cost more than twice as much. The Fujifilm X-T5 is the most capable and one of the most pleasurable APS-C cameras for still photographers in 2023 due to its class-leading high-resolution sensor, time-tested and well-honed design, and competent autofocus system, which we hope has firmware-based improvement potential. The additional functionalities, including the in-body image stabilization and higher resolution sensor, provide an additional degree of adaptability that has already demonstrated its utility. If you're in the market for a camera upgrade and desire high-end specifications packed into a small, reasonably priced body that also looks fantastic, this camera could be ideal for you.

INDEX

D

E

F

G

N

S

T

U

V

W

X

Made in United States
Troutdale, OR
12/23/2024

27169308R00133